BIBLE WISDOM FOR Fathers

COMPILED BY GARY WILDE

Christian Parenting
B O O K S

Christian Parenting Books is an imprint of Chariot Family Publishing, a division of David C. Cook Publishing Co., Elgin, Illinois 60120 David C. Cook Publishing Co., Weston, Ontario Nova Distribution Ltd., Newton Abbot, England

Christian Parenting Today Magazine P.O. Box 850, Sisters, OR 97759 (800) 238-2221

BIBLE WISDOM FOR FATHERS
©1993 by Chariot Family Publishing

Cover design by Foster Design Associates
Interior Design by Glass House Graphics
Compiled by Gary Wilde

First Printing, 1993   ISBN 0-78140-074-0
Printed in the United States of America
97 96 95 94 93 5 4 3 2

TABLE OF CONTENTS

- I Am the Light of the World
- I Am the Gate of Salvation
- I Am the Good Shepherd
- I Am the Resurrection and the Life
- I Am the Way, the Truth, the Life
- I Am the True Vine

Jesus Is Our Mentor
- Our Leader / Shepherd
- Our Example
- Our Prayer Partner: He Prays for Us
- He Understands Our Temptation

Jesus Is God
- He Claimed to Be Deity
- He Did Miracles
- Yet, He Shared Our Human Nature
- He Bore Our Sins

'How can I hold onto the joy of being a dad in the midst of home and work and stresses?'

Dealing with Your Home and Work Stresses
- When Dad Is Content with His Work
- When Dad is Content at home
- Taking Time for Rest and Renewal

Maintaining Your Spiritual Health
- Asking God to Meet Your Needs
- Finding Comfort through Christian Friends
- Lifting Your Spirit with Praise to God

Delighting In Your Children
- Let Your Enthusiasm Flow!

CHAPTER 1

'Suppose I never had a good, loving father of my own for a role model?'

I've always heard that to be a good father, you need to have had a good father yourself," said Frank. "But for some of us that's not possible, because our dads died early on, or they were abusive, or maybe they were just gone most of the time.

"But I'm thinking more lately about God as my Father. I want to be able to see Him as filling a gap in my life that was left when my dad died. I suppose even a good human father falls short in many ways, so looking to God for fathering would be a good idea for any dad who wants to do a better job of caring for his own kids."

11

FOR MEMORY:

"I will not leave you as orphans; I will come to you."

John 14:8

FOR SILENT REFLECTION:

- *In what ways have I harbored resentment toward my human father for not being "perfect"?*

- *What could I do to make peace with my human father, whether he's alive or not?*

- *How can I learn to trust my heavenly Father with more of my life, day by day?*

- *What things have I learned from my human father and from my heavenly Father that I can pass on to my own children?*

God Cares for the Fatherless

A father to the fatherless, a defender of widows, is God in his holy dwelling.

Psalm 68:5

He will call out to me, 'You are my Father, my God, the Rock my Savior.'

Psalm 89:26

Yet, O LORD, you are our Father. We are the clay, you are the potter; we are all the work of your hand.

Psalm 64:8

I will be a Father to you, and you will be my sons and daughters, says the Lord Almighty."

2 Corinthians 6:18

How great is the love the Father has lavished on us, that we should be called children of God! And that is what we are! The reason the world does not know us is that it did not know him.

1 John 3:1

He Answers Your Requests

But when you pray, go into your room, close the door and pray to your Father, who is unseen. Then your Father, who sees what is done in secret, will

13

reward you. And when you pray, do not keep on babbling like pagans, for they think they will be heard because of their many words. Do not be like them, for your Father knows what you need before you ask him. This, then, is how you should pray:

Our Father in heaven, hallowed be your name, your kingdom come, your will be done on earth as it is in heaven. Give us today our daily bread. Forgive us our debts, as we also have forgiven our debtors. And lead us not into temptation, but deliver us from the evil one.

Matthew 6:6-13

And I will do whatever you ask in my name, so that the Son may bring glory to the Father. You may ask me for anything in my name, and I will do it. If you love me, you will obey what I command. And I will ask the Father, and he will give you another Counselor to be with you forever— the Spirit of truth. The world cannot accept him, because it neither sees him nor knows him. But you know him, for he lives with you and will be in you.

John 14:13-17

He Helps You Gain Courage in Tough Situations

I am sending you out like sheep among wolves. Therefore be as shrewd as snakes and as innocent as doves. Be on your guard against men; they will hand you over to the local councils and flog you in their synagogues. On my account you will be brought before governors and kings as witnesses to them and to the Gentiles. But when they arrest you, do not worry about what to say or how to say it. At that time you will be given what to say, for it will not be you speaking, but the Spirit of your Father speaking through you.

Matthew 10:16-20

He Protects and Encourages You

See that you do not look down on one of these little ones. For I tell you that their angels in heaven always see the face of my Father in heaven.

Matthew 18:10

What do you think? If a man owns a hundred sheep, and one of them wanders away, will he not leave the ninety-nine on the hills and go to look for the one that wandered off? And if he finds it, I tell you the truth, he is happier about that one sheep than about the ninety-nine that did not wander off. In the same way your Father in heaven is not willing that any of these little ones should be lost.

Matthew 18:11-14

15

He Gives You Good Gifts

Then he said to them, "Suppose one of you has a friend, and he goes to him at midnight and says, 'Friend, lend me three loaves of bread, because a friend of mine on a journey has come to me, and I have nothing to set before him.'

Then the one inside answers, 'Don't bother me. The door is already locked, and my children are with me in bed. I can't get up and give you anything.' I tell you, though he will not get up and give him the bread because he is his friend, yet because of the man's boldness he will get up and give him as much as he needs.

So I say to you: Ask and it will be given to you; seek and you will find; knock and the door will be opened to you. For everyone who asks receives; he who seeks finds; and to him who knocks, the door will be opened. Which of you fathers, if your son asks for a fish, will give him a snake instead? Or if he asks for an egg, will give him a scorpion? If you then, though you are evil, know how to give good gifts to your children, how much more will your Father in heaven give the Holy Spirit to those who ask him!

Luke 11:5-13

Every good and perfect gift is from above, coming down from the Father of the heavenly lights, who does not change like shifting shadows.

James 1:17

He Prepares a Place for You

In my Father's house are many rooms; if it were not so, I would have told you. I am going there to prepare a place for you. And if I go and prepare a place for you, I will come back and take you to be with me that you also may be where I am. You know the way to the place where I am going.

Thomas said to him, "Lord, we don't know where you are going, so how can we know the way?" Jesus answered, "I am the way and the truth and the life. No one comes to the Father except through me. If you really knew me, you would know my Father as well. From now on, you do know him and have seen him."

Philip said, "Lord, show us the Father and that will be enough for us."

Jesus answered: "Don't you know me, Philip, even after I have been among you such a long time? Anyone who has seen me has seen the Father. How can you say, 'Show us the Father'? Don't you believe that I am in the Father, and that the Father is in me? The words I say to you are not just my own. Rather, it is the Father, living in me, who is doing his work. Believe me when I say that I am in the Father and the Father is in me; or at least believe on the evidence of the miracles themselves. I tell you the truth, anyone who has faith in me will do what I have been doing. He will do even greater things than these, because I am going to the Father.

John 14:2-12

He Chose You for Himself

Praise be to the God and Father of our Lord Jesus Christ, who has blessed us in the heavenly realms with every spiritual blessing in Christ. For he chose us in him before the creation of the world to be holy and blameless in his sight. In love he predestined us to be adopted as his sons through Jesus Christ, in accordance with his pleasure and will— to the praise of his glorious grace, which he has freely given us in the One he loves. In him we have redemption through his blood, the forgiveness of sins, in accordance with the riches of God's grace that he lavished on us with all wisdom and understanding. And he made known to us the mystery of his will according to his good pleasure, which he purposed in Christ, to be put into effect when the times will have reached their fulfillment—to bring all things in heaven and on earth together under one head, even Christ.

In him we were also chosen, having been predestined according to the plan of him who works out everything in conformity with the purpose of his will, in order that we, who were the first to hope in Christ, might be for the praise of his glory. And you also were included in Christ when you heard the word of truth, the gospel of your salvation.

Having believed, you were marked in him with a seal, the promised Holy Spirit, who is a deposit guaranteeing our inheritance until the redemption of those who are God's possession—to the praise of his glory.

Ephesians 1:3-14

He Is Your Heavenly Parent

But now, O LORD, You are our Father; We are the clay, and You our potter; And we are all the work of Your hand.

Isaiah 64:8

And because you are sons, God has sent forth the Spirit of His Son into your hearts, crying out, "Abba, Father!" Therefore you are no longer a slave but a son, and if a son, then an heir of God through Christ.

Galatians 4:6-7

19

A Good and Loving Parent

Oh, how great is Your goodness,
Which You have laid up for those who fear You;
which You have prepared for those who trust in You
in the presence of the sons of men!
You shall hide them in the secret place of Your presence
From the plots of man;
You shall keep them secretly in a pavilion
From the strife of tongues.

Psalm 31:19-20

Yet He sets the poor on high, far from affliction,
And makes their families like a flock.
The righteous see it and rejoice,
And all iniquity stops its mouth.
Whoever is wise will observe these things,
And they will understand the lovingkindness of the
LORD.

Psalm 107:41-43

For I am persuaded that neither death nor life, nor
angels nor principalities nor powers, nor things present nor things to come, nor height nor depth, nor
any other created thing, shall be able to separate us
from the love of God which is in Christ Jesus our
Lord.

Romans 8:38-39

Are not two sparrows sold for a copper coin? And not one of them falls to the ground apart from your Father's will.

Matthew 10:29

Behold what manner of love the Father has bestowed on us, that we should be called children of God!

1 John 3:1a

An Accepting Parent

God, who is rich in mercy, because of His great love with which He loved us, even when we were dead in trespasses, made us alive together with Christ (by grace you have been saved), and raised us up together, and made us sit together in the heavenly places in Christ Jesus, that in the ages to come He might show the exceeding riches of His grace in His kindness toward us in Christ Jesus. For by grace you have been saved through faith, and that not of yourselves; it is the gift of God, not of works, lest anyone should boast.

Ephesians 2:4-9

In every nation whoever fears Him and works righteousness is accepted by Him.

Acts 10:35

You also, as living stones, are being built up a spiritual house, a holy priesthood, to offer up spiritual sacrifices acceptable to God through Jesus Christ.

1 Peter 2:5

Blessed be the God and Father of our Lord Jesus Christ, who has blessed us with every spiritual blessing in the heavenly places in Christ, just as He chose us in Him before the foundation of the world, that we should be holy and without blame before Him in love, having predestined us to adoption as sons by Jesus Christ to Himself, according to the good pleasure of His will, to the praise of the glory of His grace, by which He has made us accepted in the Beloved.

Ephesians 1:3-6

A Parent Who Adopts

For as many as are led by the Spirit of God, these are sons of God. For you did not receive the spirit of bondage again to fear, but you received the Spirit of adoption by whom we cry out, "Abba, Father." The Spirit Himself bears witness with our spirit that we are children of God, and if children, then heirs—heirs of God and joint heirs with Christ, if indeed we suffer with Him, that we may also be glorified together.

Romans 8:14-22

Even so we, when we were children, were in bondage under the elements of the world. But when the fullness of the time had come, God sent forth His Son, born of a woman, born under the law, to redeem those who were under the law, that we might receive the adoption as sons. And because you are sons, God has sent forth the Spirit of His Son into your hearts, crying out, "Abba, Father!" Therefore you are no longer a slave but a son, and if a son, then an heir of God through Christ.

Galatians 4:3-7

A Parent Who Offers Comfort

"I, even I, am He who comforts you. Who are you that you should be afraid of a man who will die, And of the son of a man who will be made like grass?

Isaiah 51;12

As one whom his mother comforts, so I will comfort you; And you shall be comforted.

Isaiah 66;13a

Praise the LORD!
For it is good to sing praises to our God;
For it is pleasant, and praise is beautiful.
The LORD builds up Jerusalem;
He gathers together the outcasts of Israel.

He heals the brokenhearted
And binds up their wounds. . . .

Psalm 147:1-3

For He bruises, but He binds up; He wounds, but
His hands make whole.

Job 5:18

'Therefore all those who devour you shall be
devoured; And all your adversaries, every one of
them, shall go into captivity; Those who plunder you
shall become plunder And all who prey upon you I
will make a prey. For I will restore health to you And
heal you of your wounds,' says the LORD.

Jeremiah 30:16, 17

Blessed be the God and Father of our Lord Jesus
Christ, the Father of mercies and God of all comfort,
who comforts us in all our tribulation, that we may be
able to comfort those who are in any trouble, with the
comfort with which we ourselves are comforted by
God.

2 Corinthians 1:3, 4

For we ourselves were also once foolish, disobedient, deceived, serving various lusts and pleasures,
living in malice and envy, hateful and hating one
another. But when the kindness and the love of God
our Savior toward man appeared, not by works of

righteousness which we have done, but according to His mercy He saved us, through the washing of regeneration and renewing of the Holy Spirit, whom He poured out on us abundantly through Jesus Christ our Savior, that having been justified by His grace we should become heirs according to the hope of eternal life.

Titus 3:3-7

He will feed His flock like a shepherd; He will gather the lambs with His arm, and carry them in His bosom, And gently lead those who are with young.

Isaiah 40:11

He Has Many Encouraging Names

The Lord Is Our Righteousness
In His days Judah will be saved, And Israel will dwell safely; Now this is His name by which He will be called: The LORD OUR RIGHTEOUSNESS.

Jeremiah 23:6

The Lord Makes Us Holy
Speak also to the children of Israel, saying: 'Surely My Sabbaths you shall keep, for it is a sign between Me and you throughout your generations, that you may know that I am the LORD who sanctifies you.

Exodus 31:13

25

The Lord Heals

"If you diligently heed the voice of the LORD your God and do what is right in His sight, give ear to His commandments and keep all His statutes, I will put none of the diseases on you which I have brought on the Egyptians. For I am the LORD who heals you."

Exodus 15:26

The Lord Is Our Banner

So Joshua defeated Amalek and his people with the edge of the sword. Then the LORD said to Moses, "Write this for a memorial in the book and recount it in the hearing of Joshua, that I will utterly blot out the remembrance of Amalek from under heaven." And Moses built an altar and called its name, The-LORD-Is-My-Banner."

Exodus 17:13-15

The Lord Gives Peace

So Gideon built an altar there to the LORD, and called it The-LORD-Is-Peace. To this day it is still in Ophrah of the Abiezrites.

Judges 6:24

The Lord Is Present

All the way around shall be eighteen thousand cubits; and the name of the city from that day shall be: The LORD Is There.

Ezekiel 48:35

The Lord Will Provide

And Abraham called the name of the place, The-LORD-Will-Provide; as it is said to this day, "In the Mount of The LORD it shall be provided."

Genesis 22:14

The Lord Is the Redeemer

Thus says the LORD, your Redeemer, And He who formed you from the womb: "I am the LORD, who makes all things, Who stretches out the heavens all alone, Who spreads abroad the earth by Myself."

Isaiah 44:24

The Lord is Infinite

And God said to Moses, "I AM Who I AM." And He said, "Thus you shall say to the children of Israel, 'I AM has sent me to you.'"

Exodus 3:14

FOR PERSONAL PRAYER:

Father, sometimes I feel so alienated from my human father. And I know that this hinders my relationship with my own kids. Please enfold me in your warm, loving arms that I might do the same with those wonderful gifts—the children—that you've placed in my care.

27

CHAPTER 2

'How can I really know God's will when I'm making my parenting decisions?'

A friend at work once asked me how I thought I could raise my kids according to God's will," Bill commented. "He said that in his mind 'God' was such a foggy concept. It just didn't seem practical to try to know anything about God.

"I told him: 'That's why Jesus is so important to me. Jesus shows me exactly what God is like. Just as I have a mentor at my workplace, so I have a mentor in handling my relationships.'

"Everything about Jesus, especially the ways He responded to situations when He was on earth, shows me what a man should be like and how God's will actually works in real life. I guess I'd say I need to get to know Jesus more and more—all about Him and His example for me. My way of knowing the Father in heaven is through knowing the Son who came to earth."

FOR MEMORY:

For in Christ all the fullness of the Deity lives in bodily form. . . . leaving you an example, that you should follow in his steps.

Colossians 2:9; I Peter 2:21b

FOR SILENT REFLECTION:

- *In what ways is God more than just a mental concept for me?*

- *How well would I say I know God and His will?*

- *How would knowing more about Jesus help me understand more of God's will for my parenting approach?*

- *What aspects of Jesus' personality would I like to see developing within me as I try to be a better dad?*

You Need Supernatural Help to Be a Good Dad!

It is God who arms me with strength and makes my way perfect.

2 Samuel 22:33

Every good and perfect gift is from above, coming down from the Father of the heavenly lights, who does not change like shifting shadows.

James 1:17

The God who made the world and everything in it is the Lord of heaven and earth and does not live in temples built by hands. And he is not served by human hands, as if he needed anything, because he himself gives all men life and breath and everything else. From one man he made every nation of men, that they should inhabit the whole earth; and he determined the times set for them and the exact places where they should live. God did this so that men would seek him and perhaps reach out for him and find him, though he is not far from each one of us. For in him we live and move and have our being.'

Acts 17:24-28a

Are you so foolish? After beginning with the Spirit, are you now trying to attain your goal by human effort?

Galatians 3:3

Get to Know Who Jesus Is

I Am the Bread of Life

Then Jesus declared, "I am the bread of life. He who comes to me will never go hungry, and he who believes in me will never be thirsty. But as I told you, you have seen me and still you do not believe. All that the Father gives me will come to me, and whoever comes to me I will never drive away. For I have come down from heaven not to do my will but to do the will of him who sent me. And this is the will of him who sent me, that I shall lose none of all that he has given me, but raise them up at the last day. For my Father's will is that everyone who looks to the Son and believes in him shall have eternal life, and I will raise him up at the last day."

John 6:35-40

I Am the Light of the World

When Jesus spoke again to the people, he said, "I am the light of the world. Whoever follows me will never walk in darkness, but will have the light of life."

John 8:12

As long as it is day, we must do the work of him who sent me. Night is coming, when no one can work. While I am in the world, I am the light of the world.

John 9:4, 5

I Am the Gate of Salvation

Therefore Jesus said again, "I tell you the truth, I am the gate for the sheep. All who ever came before me were thieves and robbers, but the sheep did not listen to them. I am the gate; whoever enters through me will be saved. He will come in and go out, and find pasture. The thief comes only to steal and kill and destroy; I have come that they may have life, and have it to the full.

John 10:7-10

I Am the Good Shepherd

"I am the good shepherd. The good shepherd lays down his life for the sheep. The hired hand is not the shepherd who owns the sheep. So when he sees the wolf coming, he abandons the sheep and runs away. Then the wolf attacks the flock and scatters it. The man runs away because he is a hired hand and cares nothing for the sheep. "I am the good shepherd; I know my sheep and my sheep know me—just as the Father knows me and I know the Father—and I lay down my life for the sheep. I have other sheep that are not of this sheep pen. I must bring them also. They too will listen to my voice, and there shall be one flock and one shepherd. The reason my Father loves me is that I lay down my life—only to take it up again. No one takes it from me, but I lay it down of my own accord. I have authority to lay it

33

down and authority to take it up again. This command I received from my Father."

John 10:11-18

I Am the Resurrection and the Life

"Lord," Martha said to Jesus, "if you had been here, my brother would not have died. But I know that even now God will give you whatever you ask." Jesus said to her, "Your brother will rise again." Martha answered, "I know he will rise again in the resurrection at the last day." Jesus said to her, "I am the resurrection and the life. He who believes in me will live, even though he dies; and whoever lives and believes in me will never die. Do you believe this?"

John 11:21-26

I Am the Way, the Truth, the Life

Jesus answered, "I am the way and the truth and the life. No one comes to the Father except through me.

John 14:6

I Am the True Vine

"I am the true vine, and my Father is the gardener. He cuts off every branch in me that bears no fruit, while every branch that does bear fruit he prunes so that it will be even more fruitful. You are already clean because of the word I have spoken to you.

Remain in me, and I will remain in you. No branch can bear fruit by itself; it must remain in the vine. Neither can you bear fruit unless you remain in me. I am the vine; you are the branches. If a man remains in me and I in him, he will bear much fruit; apart from me you can do nothing. If anyone does not remain in me, he is like a branch that is thrown away and withers; such branches are picked up, thrown into the fire and burned. If you remain in me and my words remain in you, ask whatever you wish, and it will be given you.

John 15:1-7

Jesus Is Our Mentor

Our Leader / Shepherd
He tends his flock like a shepherd:
He gathers the lambs in his arms
and carries them close to his heart;
he gently leads those that have young.

Isaiah 40:11

He will stand and shepherd his flock in the strength of the LORD, in the majesty of the name of the LORD his God. And they will live securely, for then his greatness will reach to the ends of the earth.

Micah 5:4

When he saw the crowds, he had compassion on them, because they were harassed and helpless, like sheep without a shepherd.

Matthew 9:36

What do you think? If a man owns a hundred sheep, and one of them wanders away, will he not leave the ninety-nine on the hills and go to look for the one that wandered off? And if he finds it, I tell you the truth, he is happier about that one sheep than about the ninety-nine that did not wander off.

Matthew 18:12-13

And when the Chief Shepherd appears, you will receive the crown of glory that will never fade away.

1 Peter 5:4

The LORD their God will save them
on that day as the flock of his people.
They will sparkle in his land
like jewels in a crown.

Zechariah 9:16

Then Jesus told them, "This very night you will all fall away on account of me, for it is written: "'I will strike the shepherd, and the sheep of the flock will be scattered..'

Matthew 26:31

Our Example

As you sent me into the world, I have sent them into the world.

John 17:18

Take my yoke upon you and learn from me, for I am gentle and humble in heart, and you will find rest for your souls.

Matthew 11:29

You call me 'Teacher' and 'Lord,' and rightly so, for that is what I am.

John 13:13

A new command I give you: Love one another. As I have loved you, so you must love one another.

John 13:34

Each of us should please his neighbor for his good, to build him up.

Romans 15:2

Live a life of love, just as Christ loved us and gave himself up for us as a fragrant offering and sacrifice to God.

Ephesians 5:2

37

Your attitude should be the same as that of Christ Jesus: Who, being in very nature God, did not consider equality with God something to be grasped, but made himself nothing, taking the very nature of a servant, being made in human likeness. And being found in appearance as a man, he humbled himself and became obedient to death—even death on a cross!

Philippians 2:5-8

Our Prayer Partner: He Prays for Us
But I have prayed for you, Simon, that your faith may not fail. And when you have turned back, strengthen your brothers."

Luke 22:32

I pray for them. I am not praying for the world, but for those you have given me, for they are yours. All I have is yours, and all you have is mine. And glory has come to me through them. I will remain in the world no longer, but they are still in the world, and I am coming to you. Holy Father, protect them by the power of your name—the name you gave me—so that they may be one as we are one. While I was with them, I protected them and kept them safe by that name you gave me. None has been lost except the one doomed to destruction so that Scripture would be fulfilled. "I am coming to you now, but I say these things while I am still in the world, so that they may have the full measure of my joy within them. I have given them your word and the world has hated them, for they are not of the world any more than I am of the world. My prayer is not that you take them out of the world but that you protect them from the evil one.

John 17:9-15

Therefore he is able to save completely those who come to God through him, because he always lives to intercede for them.

Hebrews 7:25

For Christ did not enter a man-made sanctuary that was only a copy of the true one; he entered heaven itself, now to appear for us in God's presence.

Hebrews 9:24

My dear children, I write this to you so that you will not sin. But if anybody does sin, we have one who speaks to the Father in our defense—Jesus Christ, the Righteous One.

1 John 2:1

He Understands Our Temptations
For he will command his angels concerning you to guard you in all your ways; they will lift you up in

39

their hands, so that you will not strike your foot against a stone.

Psalm 91:11, 12

The tempter came to him and said, "If you are the Son of God, tell these stones to become bread." Jesus answered, "It is written: 'Man does not live on bread alone, but on every word that comes from the mouth of God.'"

Then the devil took him to the holy city and had him stand on the highest point of the temple. "If you are the Son of God," he said, "throw yourself down. For it is written: '"He will command his angels concerning you, and they will lift you up in their hands, so that you will not strike your foot against a stone.'" Jesus answered him, "It is also written: 'Do not put the Lord your God to the test.'" Again, the devil took him to a very high mountain and showed him all the kingdoms of the world and their splendor. All this I will give you," he said, "if you will bow down and worship me." Jesus said to him, "Away from me, Satan! For it is written: 'Worship the Lord your God, and serve him only.'" Then the devil left him, and angels came and attended him.

Matthew 4:3-11

Because he himself suffered when he was tempted, he is able to help those who are being tempted.

Hebrews 2:18

40

For we do not have a high priest who is unable to sympathize with our weaknesses, but we have one who has been tempted in every way, just as we are—yet was without sin.

Hebrews 4:15

Jesus Is God

But you, Bethlehem Ephrathah, though you are small among the clans of Judah, out of you will come for me one who will be ruler over Israel, whose origins are from of old, from ancient times.

Micah 5:2

In the beginning was the Word, and the Word was with God, and the Word was God. . . . The Word became flesh and made his dwelling among us. We have seen his glory, the glory of the One and Only, who came from the Father, full of grace and truth.

John 1:1, 14

Coming to his hometown, he began teaching the people in their synagogue, and they were amazed. "Where did this man get this wisdom and these miraculous powers?" they asked.

Matthew 13:54

Then Jesus came to them and said, "All authority in heaven and on earth has been given to me.

Matthew 28:18

Jesus said to them, "My Father is always at his work to this very day, and I, too, am working." For this reason the Jews tried all the harder to kill him; not only was he breaking the Sabbath, but he was even calling God his own Father, making himself equal with God.

John 5:17, 18

Yet for us there is but one God, the Father, from whom all things came and for whom we live; and there is but one Lord, Jesus Christ, through whom all things came and through whom we live.

I Corinthians 8:6

Who, being in very nature God, did not consider equality with God something to be grasped.

Philippians 2:6

Beyond all question, the mystery of godliness is great: He appeared in a body, was vindicated by the Spirit, was seen by angels, was preached among the nations, was believed on in the world, was taken up in glory.

I Timothy 3:16

While we wait for the blessed hope—the glorious appearing of our great God and Savior, Jesus Christ.

Titus 2:13

It is because of him that you are in Christ Jesus, who has become for us wisdom from God—that is, our righteousness, holiness and redemption.

I Corinthians 1:30

He Claimed to Be Deity

"Are you the one who was to come, or should we expect someone else?" Jesus replied, "Go back and report to John what you hear and see: The blind receive sight, the lame walk, those who have leprosy are cured, the deaf hear, the dead are raised, and the good news is preached to the poor. Blessed is the man who does not fall away on account of me."

Matthew 11:3-6

But Jesus remained silent. The high priest said to him, "I charge you under oath by the living God: Tell us if you are the Christ, the Son of God." "Yes, it is as you say," Jesus replied. "But I say to all of you: In the future you will see the Son of Man sitting at the right hand of the Mighty One and coming on the clouds of heaven." Then the high priest tore his clothes and said, "He has spoken blasphemy! Why

43

do we need any more witnesses? Look, now you
have heard the blasphemy.

Matthew 26:63-65

He said to them, "How foolish you are, and how
slow of heart to believe all that the prophets have
spoken! Did not the Christ have to suffer these things
and then enter his glory?" And beginning with Moses
and all the Prophets, he explained to them what was
said in all the Scriptures concerning himself.

Luke 24:25-27

The woman said, "I know that Messiah" (called
Christ) "is coming. When he comes, he will explain
everything to us." Then Jesus declared, "I who speak
to you am he."

John 4:25, 26

The Jews gathered around him, saying, "How long
will you keep us in suspense? If you are the Christ,
tell us plainly." Jesus answered, "I did tell you, but
you do not believe. The miracles I do in my
Father's name speak for me, but you do not
believe because you are not my sheep. My sheep
listen to my voice; I know them, and they follow
me. I give them eternal life, and they shall never
perish; no one can snatch them out of my hand.
My Father, who has given them to me, is greater

than all; no one can snatch them out of my Father's hand. I and the Father are one."

John 10:24-30

Then Jesus cried out, "When a man believes in me, he does not believe in me only, but in the one who sent me. When he looks at me, he sees the one who sent me.

John 12:44, 45

If you really knew me, you would know my Father as well. From now on, you do know him and have seen him." Philip said, "Lord, show us the Father and that will be enough for us." Jesus answered: "Don't you know me, Philip, even after I have been among you such a long time? Anyone who has seen me has seen the Father. How can you say, 'Show us the Father'? Don't you believe that I am in the Father, and that the Father is in me? The words I say to you are not just my own. Rather, it is the Father, living in me, who is doing his work.

John 14:7-10

He Did Miracles
Jesus went through all the towns and villages, teaching in their synagogues, preaching the good news of the kingdom and healing every disease and sickness.

Matthew 9:35

45

One day as Jesus was standing by the Lake of Gennesaret, with the people crowding around him and listening to the word of God, he saw at the water's edge two boats, left there by the fishermen, who were washing their nets. He got into one of the boats, the one belonging to Simon, and asked him to put out a little from shore. Then he sat down and taught the people from the boat. When he had finished speaking, he said to Simon, "Put out into deep water, and let down the nets for a catch." Simon answered, "Master, we've worked hard all night and haven't caught anything. But because you say so, I will let down the nets." When they had done so, they caught such a large number of fish that their nets began to break. So they signaled their partners in the other boat to come and help them, and they came and filled both boats so full that they began to sink. When Simon Peter saw this, he fell at Jesus' knees and said, "Go away from me, Lord; I am a sinful man!" For he and all his companions were astonished at the catch of fish they had taken, and so were James and John, the sons of Zebedee, Simon's partners. Then Jesus said to Simon, "Don't be afraid; from now on you will catch men." So they pulled their boats up on shore, left everything and followed him.

Luke 5:1-11

One who was there had been an invalid for thirty-eight years. When Jesus saw him lying there and learned that he had been in this condition for a long time, he asked him, "Do you want to get well?" "Sir," the invalid replied, "I have no one to help me into the pool when the water is stirred. While I am trying to get in, someone else goes down ahead of me." Then Jesus said to him, "Get up! Pick up your mat and walk." At once the man was cured; he picked up his mat and walked. The day on which this took place was a Sabbath.

John 5:5-9

He spit on the ground, made some mud with the saliva, and put it on the man's eyes. "Go," he told him, "wash in the Pool of Siloam" (this word means Sent). So the man went and washed, and came home seeing. His neighbors and those who had formerly seen him begging asked, "Isn't this the same man who used to sit and beg?" Some claimed that he was. Others said, "No, he only looks like him." But he himself insisted, "I am the man." "How then were your eyes opened?" they demanded. He replied, "The man they call Jesus made some mud and put it on my eyes. He told me to go to Siloam and wash. So I went and washed, and then I could see."

John 9:6b-11

Yet, He Shared Our Human Nature

Since the children have flesh and blood, he too shared in their humanity so that by his death he might destroy him who holds the power of death—that is, the devil— and free those who all their lives were held in slavery by their fear of death. For surely it is not angels he helps, but Abraham's descendants. For this reason he had to be made like his brothers in every way, in order that he might become a merciful and faithful high priest in service to God, and that he might make atonement for the sins of the people. Because he himself suffered when he was tempted, he is able to help those who are being tempted.

Hebrews 2:14-18

He Bore Our Sins

Therefore I will give him a portion among the great, and he will divide the spoils with the strong, because he poured out his life unto death, and was numbered with the transgressors. For he bore the sin of many, and made intercession for the transgressors.

Isaiah 53:12

God made him who had no sin to be sin for us, so that in him we might become the righteousness of God.

II Corinthians 5:21

He himself bore our sins in his body on the tree, so that we might die to sins and live for righteousness; by his wounds you have been healed. For you were like sheep going astray, but now you have returned to the Shepherd and Overseer of your souls.

1 Peter 2:24, 25

Therefore, brothers, since we have confidence to enter the Most Holy Place by the blood of Jesus, by a new and living way opened for us through the curtain, that is, his body, and since we have a great priest over the house of God, let us draw near to God with a sincere heart in full assurance of faith, having our hearts sprinkled to cleanse us from a guilty conscience and having our bodies washed with pure water.

Hebrews 10:19-22

FOR PERSONAL PRAYER:

Heavenly Father, I praise You for revealing Yourself through Your Son, Jesus. So many people think of 'God' as just an impersonal force that has no bearing on real life. But You've shown me, Lord, that You want me in a close, caring, personal relationship with You.

Help me learn to live as Jesus lived, and to love my children with His brand of unconditional love. Amen.

CHAPTER 3

'How can I build my home on a solid foundation of spiritual truth?'

I really don't see much in our society these days that offers a firm footing for my kids," said Sherman. "Not in terms of the kinds of values and goals I'd like to see them develop. So I've tried to go right back to the Bible. I find something solid to build on there.

"I can see that, just as we had the foundation and the bricks and mortar laid down on this house, step by step, I've got to keep laying down the basic precepts of God's wisdom for my family. Each layer of those spiritual building blocks makes my home and family life stronger. And, as an added benefit, my

51

home becomes a happier place to live!"

FOR MEMORY:
For every house is built by someone, but God is the builder of everything.

Hebrews 3:4

FOR SILENT REFLECTION:

- *How do my spiritual priorities fit into my plans for family happiness?*

- *What would my children say is my most important goal for this family?*

- *So far, how well have I conveyed my personal faith in God to my children?*

- *What part of the spiritual foundation of our family needs a little shoring up at this point?*

Building Your Home on a Solid Foundation

By wisdom a house is built, and through understanding it is established.

Proverbs 24:3

He will be the sure foundation for your times, a rich store of salvation and wisdom and knowledge; the fear of the LORD is the key to this treasure.

Isaiah 33:6

"Therefore everyone who hears these words of mine and puts them into practice is like a wise man who built his house on the rock. The rain came down, the streams rose, and the winds blew and beat against that house; yet it did not fall, because it had its foundation on the rock.

But everyone who hears these words of mine and does not put them into practice is like a foolish man who built his house on sand. The rain came down, the streams rose, and the winds blew and beat against that house, and it fell with a great crash."

When Jesus had finished saying these things, the crowds were amazed at his teaching.

Matthew 7:24-28

For no one can lay any foundation other than the one already laid, which is Jesus Christ. If any man

53

builds on this foundation using gold, silver, costly stones, wood, hay or straw, his work will be shown for what it is, because the Day will bring it to light. It will be revealed with fire, and the fire will test the quality of each man's work. If what he has built survives, he will receive his reward.

I Corinthians 3:11-14

You also, like living stones, are being built into a spiritual house to be a holy priesthood, offering spiritual sacrifices acceptable to God through Jesus Christ.

I Peter 2:5

Maintaining God-Centered Priorities

Drawing on God's Strength for Good Parenting
He gives strength to the weary and increases the power of the weak.

Isaiah 40:29

In the same way, the Spirit helps us in our weakness. We do not know what we ought to pray for, but the Spirit himself intercedes for us with groans that words cannot express.

Romans 8:26

That is why, for Christ's sake, I delight in weakness-

es, in insults, in hardships, in persecutions, in difficulties. For when I am weak, then I am strong.

II Corinthians 12:10

We are glad whenever we are weak but you are
strong; and our prayer is for your perfection.

II Corinthians 13:9

Following Christ, Your Greatest Responsibilty

What good will it be for a man if he gains the whole
world, yet forfeits his soul? Or what can a man give
in exchange for his soul?

Matthew 16:26

Jesus replied: "A certain man was preparing a great
banquet and invited many guests. At the time of the
banquet he sent his servant to tell those who had been
invited, 'Come, for everything is now ready.'

"But they all alike began to make excuses. The first
said, 'I have just bought a field, and I must go and see
it. Please excuse me.' "Another said, 'I have just bought
five yoke of oxen, and I'm on my way to try them out.
Please excuse me.' "Still another said, 'I just got married, so I can't come.'

"The servant came back and reported this to his
master. Then the owner of the house became angry
and ordered his servant, 'Go out quickly into the
streets and alleys of the town and bring in the poor,

the crippled, the blind and the lame.' "'Sir,' the servant said, 'what you ordered has been done, but there is still room.'

"Then the master told his servant, 'Go out to the roads and country lanes and make them come in, so that my house will be full. I tell you, not one of those men who were invited will get a taste of my banquet.'"

Luke 14:16-25

Making Tough Decisions

Anyone who loves his father or mother more than me is not worthy of me; anyone who loves his son or daughter more than me is not worthy of me; and anyone who does not take his cross and follow me is not worthy of me. Whoever finds his life will lose it, and whoever loses his life for my sake will find it.

Matthew 10:37-39

As they were walking along the road, a man said to him, "I will follow you wherever you go." Jesus replied, "Foxes have holes and birds of the air have nests, but the Son of Man has no place to lay his head."

He said to another man, "Follow me." But the man replied, "Lord, first let me go and bury my father." Jesus said to him, "Let the dead bury their own dead, but you go and proclaim the kingdom of God." Still another said, "I will follow you, Lord; but first let me go back and say good-by to my family."

Jesus replied, "No one who puts his hand to the plow and looks back is fit for service in the kingdom of God."

Luke 9:57-62

Planning for the Things that Last

And he told them this parable: "The ground of a certain rich man produced a good crop. He thought to himself, 'What shall I do? I have no place to store my crops.'

"Then he said, 'This is what I'll do. I will tear down my barns and build bigger ones, and there I will store all my grain and my goods. And I'll say to myself, "You have plenty of good things laid up for many years. Take life easy; eat, drink and be merry."

"But God said to him, 'You fool! This very night your life will be demanded from you. Then who will get what you have prepared for yourself?' "This is how it will be with anyone who stores up things for himself but is not rich toward God."

Luke 12:16-21

The man who loves his life will lose it, while the man who hates his life in this world will keep it for eternal life.

John 12:25

Do not deceive yourselves. If any one of you thinks

57

he is wise by the standards of this age, he should become a "fool" so that he may become wise. For the wisdom of this world is foolishness in God's sight. As it is written: "He catches the wise in their craftiness."

I Corinthians 3:18, 19

May I never boast except in the cross of our Lord Jesus Christ, through which the world has been crucified to me, and I to the world.

Galatians 6:14

Since you died with Christ to the basic principles of this world, why, as though you still belonged to it, do you submit to its rules?

Colossians 2:20

The kingdom of the world has become the kingdom of our Lord and of his Christ, and he will reign for ever and ever.

Revelation 11:15

Taking Jesus' Warnings Seriously
Do not be afraid of those who kill the body but cannot kill the soul. Rather, be afraid of the One who can destroy both soul and body in hell.

Matthew 10:28

Jesus told them another parable: "The kingdom of heaven is like a man who sowed good seed in his field. But while everyone was sleeping, his enemy came and sowed weeds among the wheat, and went away. When the wheat sprouted and formed heads, then the weeds also appeared.

"The owner's servants came to him and said, 'Sir, didn't you sow good seed in your field? Where then did the weeds come from?' "'An enemy did this,' he replied. "The servants asked him, 'Do you want us to go and pull them up?' "'No,' he answered, 'because while you are pulling the weeds, you may root up the wheat with them. Let both grow together until the harvest. At that time I will tell the harvesters: First collect the weeds and tie them in bundles to be burned; then gather the wheat and bring it into my barn.'"

Matthew 13:24-30

"Once again, the kingdom of heaven is like a net that was let down into the lake and caught all kinds of fish. When it was full, the fishermen pulled it up on the shore.

Then they sat down and collected the good fish in baskets, but threw the bad away. This is how it will be at the end of the age. The angels will come and separate the wicked from the righteous and throw them into the fiery furnace, where there will be weeping and gnashing of teeth.

Matthew 13:47-50

Accepting God's Sovereignty in All Things

"O Sovereign LORD, you have begun to show to
your servant your greatness and your strong hand.
For what god is there in heaven or on earth who can
do the deeds and mighty works you do?

Deuteronomy 3:24

Then the LORD spoke to Job out of the storm:
"Brace yourself like a man;
I will question you,
and you shall answer me.
Would you discredit my justice?
Would you condemn me to justify yourself?
Do you have an arm like God's,
and can your voice thunder like his?
Then adorn yourself with glory and splendor,
and clothe yourself in honor and majesty.
Unleash the fury of your wrath,
look at every proud man and bring him low,
look at every proud man and humble him,
crush the wicked where they stand.
Bury them all in the dust together;
shroud their faces in the grave.
Then I myself will admit to you
that your own right hand can save you.

Job 40:6-14

The heavens are yours, and yours also the earth; you founded the world and all that is in it.

Psalm 89:11

By wisdom the LORD laid the earth's foundations,
by understanding he set the heavens in place;
By his knowledge the deeps were divided,
and the clouds let drop the dew.

Proverbs 3:19, 20

For a man's ways are in full view of the LORD, and he examines all his paths.

Proverbs 5:21

Death and Destruction lie open before the LORD—
how much more the hearts of men!

Proverbs 15:11

Bequeathing Spiritual Priorities to Your Kids

Teaching Your Kids to Love the Word of God
Do not let this Book of the Law depart from your mouth; meditate on it day and night, so that you may be careful to do everything written in it. Then you will be prosperous and successful.

Joshua 1:8

61

On my bed I remember you; I think of you through the watches of the night.

Psalm 63:6

I will meditate on all your works and consider all your mighty deeds.

Psalm 77:12

I have hidden your word in my heart
that I might not sin against you. . . .
I delight in your decrees;
I will not neglect your word. . . .
Then I will answer the one who taunts me,
for I trust in your word. . . .
My comfort in my suffering is this:
Your promise preserves my life.

Psalm 119:11-50

I remember the days of long ago; I meditate on all your works and consider what your hands have done.

Psalm 143:5

Your word is a lamp to my feet
and a light for my path. . . .
Sustain me according to your promise,
and I will live; do not let my hopes be dashed. . . .
Direct my footsteps according to your word;

let no sin rule over me. . . .
Your promises have been thoroughly tested,
and your servant loves them. . . .
I rise before dawn and cry for help;
I have put my hope in your word.
My eyes stay open
through the watches of the night,
that I may meditate on your promises. . . .

Psalm 119:105-148

Finally, brothers, whatever is true, whatever is noble, whatever is right, whatever is pure, whatever is lovely, whatever is admirable—if anything is excellent or praiseworthy—think about such things.

Philippians 4:8

For the word of God is living and active. Sharper than any double-edged sword, it penetrates even to dividing soul and spirit, joints and marrow; it judges the thoughts and attitudes of the heart. Nothing in all creation is hidden from God's sight Everything is uncovered and laid bare before the eyes of him to whom we must give account.

Hebrews 4:12, 13

Be diligent in these matters; give yourself wholly to them, so that everyone may see your progress.

I Timothy 4:15

63

All Scripture is God-breathed and is useful for teaching, rebuking, correcting and training in righteousness.So that the man of God may be thoroughly equipped for every good work.

II Timothy 3:16, 17

Helping Your Kids Find Personal Salvation

Come to me, all you who are weary and burdened, and I will give you rest. Take my yoke upon you and learn from me, for I am gentle and humble in heart, and you will find rest for your souls. For my yoke is easy and my burden is light.

Matthew 11:28-30

At that time the disciples came to Jesus and asked, "Who is the greatest in the kingdom of heaven?" He called a little child and had him stand among them. And he said: "I tell you the truth, unless you change and become like little children, you will never enter the kingdom of heaven.

Therefore, whoever humbles himself like this child is the greatest in the kingdom of heaven. And whoever welcomes a little child like this in my name welcomes me. But if anyone causes one of these little ones who believe in me to sin, it would be better for him to have a large millstone hung around his neck and to be drowned in the depths of the sea.

Matthew 18:1-10

You see, at just the right time, when we were still powerless, Christ died for the ungodly.

Very rarely will anyone die for a righteous man, though for a good man someone might possibly dare to die. But God demonstrates his own love for us in this:

While we were still sinners, Christ died for us. Since we have now been justified by his blood, how much more shall we be saved from God's wrath through him! For if, when we were God's enemies, we were reconciled to him through the death of his Son, how much more, having been reconciled, shall we be saved through his life!

Romans 5:6-10

[So] if you confess with your mouth, "Jesus is Lord," and believe in your heart that God raised him from the dead, you will be saved. For it is with your heart that you believe and are justified, and it is with your mouth that you confess and are saved.

Romans 10:9, 10

Teaching Your Kids the Greatness of God

He Is All-Powerful

Yours, O LORD, is the greatness and the power and the glory and the majesty and the splendor, for everything in heaven and earth is yours. Yours, O LORD, is the kingdom; you are exalted as head over all. Wealth and honor come from you; you are the ruler of all things. In your hands are strength and power to exalt and give strength to all.

II Chronicles 29:11, 12

The LORD is my strength and my shield;
my heart trusts in him, and I am helped.
My heart leaps for joy
and I will give thanks to him in song.
The LORD is the strength of his people,
a fortress of salvation for his anointed one.

Psalm 28:7, 8

The LORD is slow to anger and great in power;
the LORD will not leave the guilty unpunished.
His way is in the whirlwind and the storm,
and clouds are the dust of his feet.
He rebukes the sea and dries it up;
he makes all the rivers run dry.
Bashan and Carmel wither

and the blossoms of Lebanon fade.
The mountains quake before him
and the hills melt away.
The earth trembles at his presence,
the world and all who live in it.
Who can withstand his indignation?
Who can endure his fierce anger?
His wrath is poured out like fire;
the rocks are shattered before him.

Nahum 1:3-6

What, then, shall we say in response to this? If God
is for us, who can be against us?

Romans 8:31

He Is All-Knowing and Wise

By his knowledge the deeps were divided, and the
clouds let drop the dew.

Proverbs 3:20

The LORD brought me, [Wisdom], forth as the first of
his works,
before his deeds of old; I was appointed from eterni-
ty,
from the beginning, before the world began.
When there were no oceans, I was given birth,
when there were no springs abounding with water;
before the mountains were settled in place,

67

before the hills, I was given birth,
before he made the earth or its fields
or any of the dust of the world.
I was there when he set the heavens in place,
when he marked out the horizon
on the face of the deep,
when he established the clouds above
and fixed securely the fountains of the deep,
  when he gave the sea its boundary so the waters
would not overstep his command,
and when he marked out the foundations of the
earth.
Then I was the craftsman at his side.
I was filled with delight day after day, rejoicing
always in his presence,
rejoicing in his whole world and delighting in
mankind.

Proverbs 8:22-31

And even the very hairs of your head are all numbered.

Matthew 10:30

He Seeks Faithful Worshipers

Now faith is being sure of what we hope for and certain of what we do not see. This is what the ancients
were commended for. By faith we understand that

the universe was formed at God's command, so that what is seen was not made out of what was visible. By faith Abel offered God a better sacrifice than Cain did. By faith he was commended as a righteous man, when God spoke well of his offerings. And by faith he still speaks, even though he is dead. By faith Enoch was taken from this life, so that he did not experience death; he could not be found, because God had taken him away. For before he was taken, he was commended as one who pleased God. And without faith it is impossible to please God, because anyone who comes to him must believe that he exists and that he rewards those who earnestly seek him.

Hebrews 11:1-6

FOR PERSONAL PRAYER:

Lord, remind me that only You can provide a firm, lasting foundation for my family's growth. Give me a greater desire for Your righteousness and wisdom as I seek to build a home that honors You in every way. Amen.

CHAPTER 4

'How can I keep my family life healthy when so many forces work to break it down?'

Somebody asked me once: 'What, really, is a healthy family?'

"It got me to thinking," said Andy. "I know what a healthy person is, and what a sick person is. So I think a healthy family is one in which all the parts are working together. Then the whole family fulfills it's God-given potential. In a sick family the relationships have weakened, coordination is out of sync, and communication has broken down. And maybe the temperature between Mom and Dad starts cooling to a dangerous level.

"That's a tough situation for the kids. Yet, as a

Christian, I know God will continue to work in a family no matter what the current diagnosis. God always works for the healing of hurts."

FOR MEMORY:

But for you who revere my name, the sun of righteousness will rise with healing in its wings.

Malachi 4:2a

FOR SILENT REFLECTION:

- *What's healthy and unhealthy about my family life right now?*

- *In what specific ways have I been contributing to my family's health?*

- *What practical step could I take to bring healing to the hurts I find in my wife and children?*

Keep the Home Happy for Your Children

A Place Where God is Loved

Know therefore that the LORD your God is God; he is the faithful God, keeping his covenant of love to a thousand generations of those who love him and keep his commands.

Deuteronomy 7:9

Delight yourself in the LORD and he will give you the desires of your heart.

Psalm 37:4

The LORD watches over all who love him, but all the wicked he will destroy.

Psalm 145:20

I love those who love me, and those who seek me find me.

Proverbs 8:17

Whoever has my commands and obeys them, he is the one who loves me. He who loves me will be loved by my Father, and I too will love him and show myself to him."

John 14:21

No eye has seen, no ear has heard, no mind has conceived what God has prepared for those who love him.

I Corinthians 2:9

A Place Where God Provides the Ultimate Security
He provides food for those who fear him; he remembers his covenant forever.

Psalm 111:5

I will bless her with abundant provisions; her poor will I satisfy with food.

Psalm 132:15

You will have plenty to eat, until you are full, and you will praise the name of the LORD your God, who has worked wonders for you; never again will my people be shamed.

Joel 2:26

You care for the land and water it; you enrich it abundantly. The streams of God are filled with water to provide the people with grain, for so you have ordained it.

Psalm 65:9

Do you think I cannot call on my Father, and he will at once put at my disposal more than twelve legions of angels?

Matthew 26:53

A Place of Christian Hospitality

For I was hungry and you gave me something to eat, I was thirsty and you gave me something to drink, I was a stranger and you invited me in, I needed clothes and you clothed me, I was sick and you looked after me, I was in prison and you came to visit me.' "The King will reply, 'I tell you the truth, whatever you did for one of the least of these brothers of mine, you did for me.'

Matthew 25:35-40

I tell you the truth, anyone who gives you a cup of water in my name because you belong to Christ will certainly not lose his reward.

Mark 9:41

In everything I did, I showed you that by this kind of hard work we must help the weak, remembering the words the Lord Jesus himself said: 'It is more blessed to give than to receive.'"

Acts 20:35

Share with God's people who are in need. Practice hospitality.

Romans 12:13

Our desire is not that others might be relieved while you are hard pressed, but that there might be equality. At the present time your plenty will supply what they need, so that in turn their plenty will supply what you need. Then there will be equality.

II Corinthians 8:13, 14

Suppose a brother or sister is without clothes and daily food. If one of you says to him, "Go, I wish you well; keep warm and well fed," but does nothing about his physical needs, what good is it?

James 2:15, 16

Offer hospitality to one another without grumbling. Each one should use whatever gift he has received to serve others, faithfully administering God's grace in its various forms.

I Peter 4:9, 10

If anyone has material possessions and sees his brother in need but has no pity on him, how can the love of God be in him?

I John 3:17

Do not forget to entertain strangers, for by so doing some people have entertained angels without knowing it.

Hebrews 13:2

A Place of Loving Communication

An offended brother is more unyielding than a fortified

city, and disputes are like the barred gates of a citadel.

Proverbs 18:19

A foolish son is his father's ruin, and a quarrelsome wife is like a constant dripping.

Proverbs 19:13

Better to live on a corner of the roof than share a house with a quarrelsome wife.

Proverbs 21:9

May the God who gives endurance and encouragement give you a spirit of unity among yourselves as you follow Christ Jesus, so that with one heart and mouth you may glorify the God and Father of our Lord Jesus Christ.

Romans 15:5, 6

Carry each other's burdens, and in this way you will fulfill the law of Christ. If anyone thinks he is something when he is nothing, he deceives himself. Each one should test his own actions. Then he can take pride in himself, without comparing himself to somebody else.

Galatians 6:2-4

Be completely humble and gentle; be patient, bearing with one another in love. Make every effort to keep

77

the unity of the Spirit through the bond of peace.

Ephesians 4:2, 3

Speaking the truth in love, we will in all things grow up into him who is the Head, that is, Christ. From him the whole body, joined and held together by every supporting ligament, grows and builds itself up in love, as each part does its work.

Ephesians 4:15, 16

Speak to one another with psalms, hymns and spiritual songs. Sing and make music in your heart to the Lord, always giving thanks to God the Father for everything, in the name of our Lord Jesus Christ.

Ephesians 5:19, 20

A Place Where Money Is Handled Faithfully

Jesus sat down opposite the place where the offerings were put and watched the crowd putting their money into the temple treasury. Many rich people threw in large amounts. But a poor widow came and put in two very small copper coins, worth only a fraction of a penny. Calling his disciples to him, Jesus said, "I tell you the truth, this poor widow has put more into the treasury than all the others. They all gave out of their wealth; but she, out of her poverty, put in everything—all she had to live on."

Mark 12:41-44

Do not be afraid, little flock, for your Father has been pleased to give you the kingdom. Sell your possessions and give to the poor. Provide purses for yourselves that will not wear out, a treasure in heaven that will not be exhausted, where no thief comes near and no moth destroys. For where your treasure is, there your heart will be also.

Luke 12:32-34

But godliness with contentment is great gain. For we brought nothing into the world, and we can take nothing out of it. But if we have food and clothing, we will be content with that. People who want to get rich fall into temptation and a trap and into many foolish and harmful desires that plunge men into ruin and destruction. For the love of money is a root of all kinds of evil. Some people, eager for money, have wandered from the faith and pierced themselves with many griefs. But you, man of God, flee from all this, and pursue righteousness, godliness, faith, love, endurance and gentleness.

I Timothy 6:6-11

A Place of Sexual Fidelity

May your fountain be blessed,
and may you rejoice in the wife of your youth.
A loving doe, a graceful deer—
may her breasts satisfy you always,

79

may you ever be captivated by her love.
Why be captivated, my son, by an adulteress?
Why embrace the bosom of another man's wife?

Proverb 5:18-20

In the same way, count yourselves dead to sin but alive to God in Christ Jesus. Therefore do not let sin reign in your mortal body so that you obey its evil desires. Do not offer the parts of your body to sin, as instruments of wickedness, but rather offer yourselves to God, as those who have been brought from death to life; and offer the parts of your body to him as instruments of righteousness. For sin shall not be your master, because you are not under law, but under grace.

Romans 6:11-14

All of us also lived among them at one time, gratifying the cravings of our sinful nature and following its desires and thoughts. Like the rest, we were by nature objects of wrath. But because of his great love for us, God, who is rich in mercy, made us alive with Christ even when we were dead in transgressions—it is by grace you have been saved. And God raised us up with Christ and seated us with him in the heavenly realms in Christ Jesus.

Ephesians 2:3-6

BIBLE WISDOM FOR FATHERS

Flee the evil desires of youth, and pursue righteousness, faith, love and peace, along with those who call on the Lord out of a pure heart.

II Timothy 2:22

Food for the stomach and the stomach for food"— but God will destroy them both. The body is not meant for sexual immorality, but for the Lord, and the Lord for the body. . . . Do you not know that your bodies are members of Christ himself? Shall I then take the members of Christ and unite them with a prostitute? Never!

I Corinthians 6:13, 15

It is God's will that you should be sanctified: that you should avoid sexual immorality.

I Thessalonians 4:3

Marriage should be honored by all, and the marriage bed kept pure, for God will judge the adulterer and all the sexually immoral.

Hebrews 13:4

A Place of Peaceful Togetherness
Make every effort to live in peace with all men and to be holy; without holiness no one will see the Lord.

Hebrews 12:14

To the married I give this command (not I, but the Lord): A wife must not separate from her husband. But if she does, she must remain unmarried or else be reconciled to her husband. And a husband must not divorce his wife. To the rest I say this (I, not the Lord):

If any brother has a wife who is not a believer and she is willing to live with him, he must not divorce her.

And if a woman has a husband who is not a believer and he is willing to live with her, she must not divorce him. For the unbelieving husband has been sanctified through his wife, and the unbelieving wife has been sanctified through her believing husband. Otherwise your children would be unclean, but as it is, they are holy.

But if the unbeliever leaves, let him do so. A believing man or woman is not bound in such circumstances; God has called us to live in peace. How do you know, wife, whether you will save your husband? Or, how do you know, husband, whether you will save your wife?

I Corinthians 7:10-16

Keep the Romance Alive before Your Children

Husbands, Adore Your Wives

How beautiful you are, my darling!
Oh, how beautiful!
Your eyes behind your veil are doves.
Your hair is like a flock of goats
descending from Mount Gilead.
Your teeth are like a flock of sheep just shorn,
coming up from the washing.
Each has its twin; not one of them is alone.
Your lips are like a scarlet ribbon;
your mouth is lovely.
Your temples behind your veil
are like the halves of a pomegranate.
Your neck is like the tower of David,
built with elegance; on it hang a thousand shields,
all of them shields of warriors.
Your two breasts are like two fawns,
like twin fawns of a gazelle that browse among the
lilies.
Until the day breaks and the shadows flee,
 I will go to the mountain of myrrh
and to the hill of incense.
All beautiful you are, my darling;
there is no flaw in you.

Song of Songs 4:1-7

83

She sees that her trading is profitable,
and her lamp does not go out at night.
In her hand she holds the distaff
and grasps the spindle with her fingers.
She opens her arms to the poor
and extends her hands to the needy.
When it snows, she has no fear for her household;
for all of them are clothed in scarlet.
She makes coverings for her bed;
she is clothed in fine linen and purple.
Her husband is respected at the city gate,
where he takes his seat among the elders of the land.
She makes linen garments and sells them,
and supplies the merchants with sashes.
She is clothed with strength and dignity;
she can laugh at the days to come.
She speaks with wisdom,
and faithful instruction is on her tongue.
She watches over the affairs of her household
and does not eat the bread of idleness.
Her children arise and call her blessed;
her husband also, and he praises her:
Many women do noble things, but you surpass them all.

Proverbs 31:18-29

Submit to one another out of reverence for Christ. . . .
Husbands, love your wives, just as Christ loved the
church and gave himself up for her to make her holy,

cleansing her by the washing with water through the word, and to present her to himself as a radiant church, without stain or wrinkle or any other blemish, but holy and blameless. In this same way, husbands ought to love their wives as their own bodies. He who loves his wife loves himself. After all, no one ever hated his own body, but he feeds and cares for it, just as Christ does the church— for we are members of his body. "For this reason a man will leave his father and mother and be united to his wife, and the two will become one flesh." This is a profound mystery—but I am talking about Christ and the church. However, each one of you also must love his wife as he loves himself.

Ephesians 5:21-33a

Husbands, in the same way be considerate as you live with your wives, and treat them with respect as the weaker partner and as heirs with you of the gracious gift of life, so that nothing will hinder your prayers.

I Peter 3:7

Consider the Consequences of Adultery
Do not lust in your heart after her beauty
or let her captivate you with her eyes,
for the prostitute reduces you to a loaf of bread,
and the adulteress preys upon your very life.
Can a man scoop fire into his lap

without his clothes being burned?
Can a man walk on hot coals
without his feet being scorched?
So is he who sleeps with another man's wife;
no one who touches her will go unpunished.

Proverbs 6:25-29

The LORD sent Nathan to David. When he came to him, he said, "There were two men in a certain town, one rich and the other poor. The rich man had a very large number of sheep and cattle, but the poor man had nothing except one little ewe lamb he had bought. He raised it, and it grew up with him and his children. It shared his food, drank from his cup and even slept in his arms. It was like a daughter to him. Now a traveler came to the rich man, but the rich man refrained from taking one of his own sheep or cattle to prepare a meal for the traveler who had come to him. Instead, he took the ewe lamb that belonged to the poor man and prepared it for the one who had come to him."

David burned with anger against the man and said to Nathan, "As surely as the LORD lives, the man who did this deserves to die! He must pay for that lamb four times over, because he did such a thing and had no pity."

Then Nathan said to David, "You are the man! This is what the LORD, the God of Israel, says: 'I anointed you king over Israel, and I delivered you from the hand of Saul. I gave your master's house to you, and your master's wives into your arms. I gave you the house of Israel and Judah. And if all this had been too little, I would have given you even more.

Why did you despise the word of the LORD by doing what is evil in his eyes? You struck down Uriah the Hittite with the sword and took his wife to be your own. You killed him with the sword of the Ammonites. Now, therefore, the sword will never depart from your house, because you despised me and took the wife of Uriah the Hittite to be your own.'

"This is what the LORD says: 'Out of your own household I am going to bring calamity upon you. Before your very eyes I will take your wives and give them to one who is close to you, and he will lie with your wives in broad daylight. You did it in secret, but I will do this thing in broad daylight before all Israel.'" Then David said to Nathan, "I have sinned against the LORD."

II Samuel 12:1-13a

You have heard that it was said, "Do not commit adultery." But I tell you that anyone who looks at a woman lustfully has already committed adultery with her in his heart.

Matthew 5:27, 28

87

FOR PERSONAL PRAYER:

Father, through Your Word I see that one of the best things I can do for my children is to love their mother. Help me learn to express my feelings of love and affection more openly. Don't let me keep my thankfulness for my family a secret any longer. Amen.

CHAPTER 5

'How can I bestow a sense of blessing on my children the way fathers did it in the Bible?'

Al mused: "I'm so impressed by how those Old Testament fathers laid blessings on their children. I mean, picture it: The father calls his child over, looks him straight in the eye, places his hand firmly on the child's head and says: 'You are fantastic, kid; and God thinks so, too.' Wow!

"In my house, most of the time I feel fortunate if I even make eye contact with my teens—or say anything at all—as they fly out the door to their next extra-curricular activity. I'm convinced I've got to slow things down a little. I need to make more time to hold my kids and say, "Daughter, I'm so proud of you. You are a joy to me, just because of who you are.

"Can you imagine what that kind of thing can do for a child's self-esteem? The last time I tried it, my youngest son seemed to be walking on a cloud for the next three days. Couldn't get the smile off his face."

FOR MEMORY:
"Bless me—me too, my father!"

Genesis 27:34b

FOR SILENT REFLECTION:

- *How much was I affirmed and blessed in my family of origin?*

- *What makes it hard or easy for me to bless my children?*

- *What forms of blessing are my children longing for right now?*

Children Crave Dad's Blessing!

After Isaac finished blessing him and Jacob had scarcely left his father's presence, his brother Esau came in from hunting. He too prepared some tasty food and brought it to his father. Then he said to him, "My father, sit up and eat some of my game, so that you may give me your blessing."

His father Isaac asked him, "Who are you?" "I am your son," he answered, "your firstborn, Esau." Isaac trembled violently and said, "Who was it, then, that hunted game and brought it to me? I ate it just before you came and I blessed him—and indeed he will be blessed!"

When Esau heard his father's words, he burst out with a loud and bitter cry and said to his father, "Bless me—me too, my father!" Esau said to his father, "Do you have only one blessing, my father? Bless me too, my father!" Then Esau wept aloud.

Genesis 27:30-38

Blessings in the Old Testament

Isaac Blesses His Son Jacob

Then his father Isaac said to him, "Come here, my son, and kiss me." So he went to him and kissed him. When Isaac caught the smell of his clothes, he blessed him and said, "Ah, the smell of my son is like the smell of a field that the LORD has blessed.

91

May God give you of heaven's dew and of earth's richness—an abundance of grain and new wine. May nations serve you and peoples bow down to you. Be lord over your brothers, and may the sons of your mother bow down to you. May those who curse you be cursed and those who bless you be blessed."

Genesis 27:23-29

So Isaac called for Jacob and blessed him and commanded him: "Do not marry a Canaanite woman. Go at once to Paddan Aram, to the house of your mother's father Bethuel. Take a wife for yourself there, from among the daughters of Laban, your mother's brother. May God Almighty bless you and make you fruitful and increase your numbers until you become a community of peoples. May he give you and your descendants the blessing given to Abraham, so that you may take possession of the land where you now live as an alien, the land God gave to Abraham."

Genesis 28:1-4

Jacob Blesses His Grandsons

When [Jacob] saw the sons of Joseph, he asked, "Who are these?" "They are the sons God has given me here," Joseph said to his father. Then Israel said, "Bring them to me so I may bless them." Now [Jacob's] eyes were failing because of old age, and he could hardly see.

So Joseph brought his sons close to him, and his father kissed them and embraced them. [Jacob] said to Joseph, "I never expected to see your face again, and now God has allowed me to see your children too." Then Joseph removed them from [Jacob's] knees and bowed down with his face to the ground. And Joseph took both of them, Ephraim on his right toward [Jacob's] left hand and Manasseh on his left toward [Jacob's] right hand, and brought them close to him. But [Jacob] reached out his right hand and put it on Ephraim's head, though he was the younger, and crossing his arms, he put his left hand on Manasseh's head, even though Manasseh was the firstborn. . . .

When Joseph saw his father placing his right hand on Ephraim's head he was displeased; so he took hold of his father's hand to move it from Ephraim's head to Manasseh's head. Joseph said to him, "No, my father, this one is the firstborn; put your right hand on his head."

But his father refused and said, "I know, my son, I know. He too will become a people, and he too will become great. Nevertheless, his younger brother will be greater than he, and his descendants will become a group of nations." He blessed them that day and said, "In your name will Israel pronounce this blessing: 'May God make you like Ephraim and Manasseh.'" So he put Ephraim ahead of Manasseh.

Genesis 48:8-20

93

Jacob Blesses His Son Joseph

Then he blessed Joseph and said, "May the God before whom my fathers Abraham and Isaac walked, the God who has been my shepherd all my life to this day, the Angel who has delivered me from all harm—may he bless these boys. May they be called by my name and the names of my fathers Abraham and Isaac, and may they increase greatly upon the earth."

Genesis 48:15, 16

Ministers Bless the People

"Tell Aaron and his sons, 'This is how you are to bless the Israelites. Say to them: The LORD bless you and keep you; the LORD make his face shine upon you and be gracious to you; the LORD turn his face toward you and give you peace." '

Numbers 6:23-26

May the God of hope fill you with all joy and peace as you trust in him, so that you may overflow with hope by the power of the Holy Spirit.

Romans 15:13

May the God of peace, who through the blood of the eternal covenant brought back from the dead our Lord Jesus, that great Shepherd of the sheep, equip you with everything good for doing his will, and may

BIBLE WISDOM FOR FATHERS

he work in us what is pleasing to him, through Jesus
Christ, to whom be glory for ever and ever. Amen.

Hebrews 13:20, 21

Grace and peace be yours in abundance through the
knowledge of God and of Jesus our Lord. His divine
power has given us everything we need for life and
godliness through our knowledge of him who called
us by his own glory and goodness. Through these he
has given us his very great and precious promises, so
that through them you may participate in the divine
nature and escape the corruption in the world
caused by evil desires.

II Peter 1:2-4

Promises of Spiritual Blessing from God

Blessed are those whose strength is in you, who
have set their hearts on pilgrimage.

Psalm 84:5

Then your light will break forth like the dawn,
and your healing will quickly appear;
then your righteousness will go before you,
and the glory of the LORD will be your rear guard.
Then you will call, and the LORD will answer;
you will cry for help, and he will say: Here am I.
"If you do away with the yoke of oppression,

95

with the pointing finger and malicious talk,
and if you spend yourselves in behalf of the hungry
and satisfy the needs of the oppressed,
then your light will rise in the darkness,
and your night will become like the noonday.
The LORD will guide you always;
he will satisfy your needs in a sun-scorched land
and will strengthen your frame.
You will be like a well-watered garden,
like a spring whose waters never fail.

Isaiah 58:8-11

They will come and shout for joy
on the heights of Zion;
they will rejoice in the bounty of the LORD—
the grain, the new wine and the oil,
the young of the flocks and herds.
They will be like a well-watered garden,
and they will sorrow no more.
Then maidens will dance and be glad,
young men and old as well.
I will turn their mourning into gladness;
I will give them comfort and joy instead of sorrow.
I will satisfy the priests with abundance,
and my people will be filled with my bounty,"
declares the LORD.

Jeremiah 31:12-14

If you then, though you are evil, know how to give good gifts to your children, how much more will your Father in heaven give the Holy Spirit to those who ask him!"

Luke 11:13

On the last and greatest day of the Feast, Jesus stood and said in a loud voice, "If anyone is thirsty, let him come to me and drink. Whoever believes in me, as the Scripture has said, streams of living water will flow from within him." By this he meant the Spirit, whom those who believed in him were later to receive. Up to that time the Spirit had not been given, since Jesus had not yet been glorified.

John 7:37-39

And I will ask the Father, and he will give you another Counselor to be with you forever—Spirit of truth. The world cannot accept him, because it neither sees him nor knows him. But you know him, for he lives with you and will be in you. . . . But the Counselor, the Holy Spirit, whom the Father will send in my name, will teach you all things and will remind you of everything I have said to you. Peace I leave with you; my peace I give you. I do not give to you as the world gives. Do not let your hearts be troubled and do not be afraid.

John 14:16, 17, 26, 27

97

Now I commit you to God and to the word of his grace, which can build you up and give you an inheritance among all those who are sanctified.

Acts 20:32

To him who is able to keep you from falling and to present you before his glorious presence without fault and with great joy—to the only God our Savior be glory, majesty, power and authority, through Jesus Christ our Lord, before all ages, now and forevermore! Amen.

Jude 1:24, 25

Promises of Temporal Blessing from God

He who dwells in the shelter of the Most High
will rest in the shadow of the Almighty.
will say of the LORD, "He is my refuge and my fortress,
my God, in whom I trust."
Surely he will save you from the fowler's snare
and from the deadly pestilence.
He will cover you with his feathers,
and under his wings you will find refuge;
his faithfulness will be your shield and rampart.
You will not fear the terror of night,
nor the arrow that flies by day,

nor the pestilence that stalks in the darkness,
nor the plague that destroys at midday.
A thousand may fall at your side,
ten thousand at your right hand,
but it will not come near you.
You will only observe with your eyes
and see the punishment of the wicked.
If you make the Most High your dwelling—
even the LORD, who is my refuge—
then no harm will befall you,
no disaster will come near your tent.
For he will command his angels concerning you
to guard you in all your ways;
they will lift you up in their hands,
so that you will not strike your foot against a stone.
You will tread upon the lion and the cobra;
you will trample the great lion and the serpent.
"Because he loves me," says the LORD,
"I will rescue him; I will protect him,
for he acknowledges my name.
He will call upon me, and I will answer him;
I will be with him in trouble,
I will deliver him and honor him.
With long life will I satisfy him
and show him my salvation."

Psalm 91:1-16

And my God will meet all your needs according to
his glorious riches in Christ Jesus.

Philippians 4:19

Scriptural Blessings to Give your Children

Blessed are you (_____Name_____),
when you do not walk in the counsel of the wicked
or stand in the way of sinners
or sit in the seat of mockers.
But your delight is in the law of the LORD,
and on his law may you meditate day and night.
Then you will be like a tree
planted by streams of water,
which yields its fruit in season
and whose leaf does not wither.
Whatever you do will prosper.
Not so the wicked!
They are like chaff that the wind blows away.
Therefore the wicked will not stand in the judgment,
nor sinners in the assembly of the righteous.
For the LORD watches over the way of the righteous,
but the way of the wicked will perish.

Psalm 1:1-6 (paraphrased)

My son/daughter, (_____Name_____),
if you accept my words
and store up my commands within you,

turning your ear to wisdom
and applying your heart to understanding,
and if you call out for insight
and cry aloud for understanding,
and if you look for it as for silver
and search for it as for hidden treasure,
then you will understand the fear of the LORD
and find the knowledge of God.
For the LORD gives wisdom,
and from his mouth come knowledge
and understanding.
He holds victory in store for the upright,
he is a shield to those whose walk is blameless,
for he guards the course of the just
and protects the way of his faithful ones.

Proverbs 2:1-8

Trust in the LORD with all your heart, (____Name____),
and lean not on your own understanding;
in all your ways acknowledge him,
and he will make your paths straight.

Proverbs 3:5, 6

I keep asking that the God of our Lord Jesus Christ, the glorious Father, may give you, (____Name____), the Spirit of wisdom and revelation, so that you may know him better.

I pray also that the eyes of your heart may be

enlightened in order that you may know the hope to which he has called you, the riches of his glorious inheritance in the saints, and his incomparably great power for us who believe.

Ephesians 1:17-23

I pray that out of his glorious riches [God] may strengthen you, (_____Name_____), with power through his Spirit in your inner being, so that Christ may dwell in your hearts through faith. And I pray that you, being rooted and established in love, may have power, together with all the saints, to grasp how wide and long and high and deep is the love of Christ, and to know this love that surpasses knowledge—that you may be filled to the measure of all the fullness of God.

Ephesians 3:16-19

FOR PERSONAL PRAYER:

Lord, I've sometimes been afraid or embarrassed to say "I love you" to my children—clearly and directly, through words and touch. Please make me more aware of the opportunities for conveying the blessing of my love for them and Your love for them. I want to see the light of that blessing shining in their eyes. Amen.

CHAPTER 6

'What values should a dad be teaching his children?'

Y ou might say I had a powerful parenting revelation the last time I filled in my income tax forms," said George. "I was facing the temptation to 'fudge' a little on a deduction. Suddenly I recalled a scene in which I was scolding little Bobby for telling a lie, and I thought to myself: Who am I really cheating here, the government, myself—or my child?

"The experience made me wake up to a crucial fact about being a dad: My child will inherit certain character traits from me just as he inerits my biological genes. That's both exciting and scary."

FOR MEMORY:

Even a child is known by his actions, by whether his conduct is pure and right.

Proverbs 20:11

FOR SILENT REFLECTION:

• *How much difference is there between the values I profess and the values I live?*

• *What character traits do I see forming in my children?*

• *In what ways are my children beginning to remind me of myself? Do these things make me mostly happy or mostly sad?*

God's Values Confront Worldly Values

Do not conform any longer to the pattern of this world, but be transformed by the renewing of your mind. Then you will be able to test and approve what God's will is—his good, pleasing and perfect will.

-Romans 12:2

Since, then, you have been raised with Christ, set your hearts on things above, where Christ is seated at the right hand of God. Set your minds on things above, not on earthly things. For you died, and your life is now hidden with Christ in God. When Christ, who is your life, appears, then you also will appear with him in glory. Put to death, therefore, whatever belongs to your earthly nature: sexual immorality, impurity, lust, evil desires and greed, which is idolatry. Because of these, the wrath of God is coming.

Colossians 3:1-6

Do not love the world or anything in the world. If anyone loves the world, the love of the Father is not in him. For everything in the world—the cravings of sinful man, the lust of his eyes and the boasting of what he has and does—comes not from the Father but from the world. The world and its desires pass away, but the man who does the will of God lives forever.

I John 2:15-17

For everyone born of God overcomes the world. This is the victory that has overcome the world, even our faith. Who is it that overcomes the world? Only he who believes that Jesus is the Son of God.

I John 5:4, 5

Therefore, prepare your minds for action; be self-controlled; set your hope fully on the grace to be given you when Jesus Christ is revealed.

I Peter 1:13

Standing for Christian Values Will Not Be Popular

If the world hates you, keep in mind that it hated me first. If you belonged to the world, it would love you as its own. As it is, you do not belong to the world, but I have chosen you out of the world. That is why the world hates you."

Remember the words I spoke to you: "No servant is greater than his master.' If they persecuted me, they will persecute you also. If they obeyed my teaching, they will obey yours also. They will treat you this way because of my name, for they do not know the One who sent me. If I had not come and spoken to them, they would not be guilty of sin. Now, however, they have no excuse for their sin. He who hates me hates my Father as well. If I had not done among them what no one else did, they would not be guilty of sin.

But now they have seen these miracles, and yet they have hated both me and my Father. But this is to fulfill what is written in their Law: "They hated me without reason."

John 15:18-25

If you are insulted because of the name of Christ, you are blessed, for the Spirit of glory and of God rests on you. If you suffer, it should not be as a murderer or thief or any other kind of criminal, or even as a meddler. However, if you suffer as a Christian, do not be ashamed, but praise God that you bear that name. For it is time for judgment to begin with the family of God; and if it begins with us, what will the outcome be for those who do not obey the gospel of God? And, "If it is hard for the righteous to be saved, what will become of the ungodly and the sinner?" So then, those who suffer according to God's will should commit themselves to their faithful Creator and continue to do good.

I Peter 4:14-19

Who is he that condemns? Christ Jesus, who died—more than that, who was raised to life—is at the right hand of God and is also interceding for us. Who shall separate us from the love of Christ? Shall trouble or hardship or persecution or famine or nakedness or danger or sword? As it is written: "For your sake we face death all day long; we are considered as sheep to be slaughtered." No, in all these things we are more than conquerors through him who loved us. For I am convinced that neither death nor life, neither angels nor demons, neither the present nor the future, nor any powers, neither height nor depth, nor anything else in all creation, will be able to separate us from the love of God that is in Christ Jesus our Lord.

Romans 8:34-39

Crucial Values to Teach Your Children

Confidence

Furious with rage, Nebuchadnezzar summoned Shadrach, Meshach and Abednego. So these men were brought before the king, and Nebuchadnezzar said to them, "Is it true, Shadrach, Meshach and Abednego, that you do not serve my gods or worship the image of gold I have set up? Now when you hear the sound of the horn, flute, zither, lyre, harp, pipes and all kinds of music, if you are ready to fall down and worship the image I made, very good. But if you do not worship it, you will be thrown immediately into a blazing furnace.

Then what god will be able to rescue you from my hand?" Shadrach, Meshach and Abednego replied to the king, "O Nebuchadnezzar, we do not need to defend ourselves before you in this matter. If we are thrown into the blazing furnace, the God we serve is able to save us from it, and he will rescue us from your hand, O king. But even if he does not, we want you to know, O king, that we will not serve your gods or worship the image of gold you have set up."

Daniel 3:13-18

I can do everything through [Christ] who gives me strength.

Philippians 4:13

Self-Discipline

But I tell you, Do not resist an evil person. If someone strikes you on the right cheek, turn to him the other also. And if someone wants to sue you and take your tunic, let him have your cloak as well. If someone forces you to go one mile, go with him two miles.

Matthew 5:39-41

Then Jesus said to his disciples, "If anyone would come after me, he must deny himself and take up his cross and follow me. For whoever wants to save his life will lose it, but whoever loses his life for me will find it. What good will it be for a man if he gains the whole world, yet forfeits his soul? Or what can a man give in exchange for his soul?

Matthew 16:24-26

Therefore, brothers, we have an obligation—but it is not to the sinful nature, to live according to it. For if you live according to the sinful nature, you will die; but if by the Spirit you put to death the misdeeds of the body, you will live.

Romans 8:12, 13

No, I beat my body and make it my slave so that after I have preached to others, I myself will not be disqualified for the prize.

I Corinthians 9:27

Those who belong to Christ Jesus have crucified the sinful nature with its passions and desires.

Galatians 5:24

For the grace of God that brings salvation has appeared to all men. It teaches us to say "No" to ungodliness and worldly passions, and to live self-controlled, upright and godly lives in this present age.

Titus 2:11, 12

Consider it pure joy, my brothers, whenever you face trials of many kinds, because you know that the testing of your faith develops perseverance. Perseverance must finish its work so that you may be mature

BIBLE WISDOM FOR FATHERS

and complete, not lacking anything.

James 1:2-4

Trustworthiness

A gossip betrays a confidence, but a trustworthy man keeps a secret.

Proverbs 11:13

Teach slaves to be subject to their masters in everything, to try to please them, not to talk back to them, and not to steal from them, but to show that they can be fully trusted, so that in every way they will make the teaching about God our Savior attractive.

Titus 2:9, 10

Compassion

As a father has compassion on his children,
so the LORD has compassion on those who fear him.

Psalm 103:13

I will plant her for myself in the land; I will show my love to the one I called "Not my loved one." I will say to those called "Not my people," "You are my people"; and they will say, "You are my God."

Hosea 2:23

On one occasion an expert in the law stood up to test Jesus. "Teacher," he asked, "what must I do to inherit eternal life?"

"What is written in the Law?" he replied. "How do you read it?"

He answered: "'Love the Lord your God with all your heart and with all your soul and with all your strength and with all your mind'; and, 'Love your neighbor as yourself.'" "You have answered correctly," Jesus replied. "Do this and you will live."

But he wanted to justify himself, so he asked Jesus, "And who is my neighbor?"

In reply Jesus said: "A man was going down from Jerusalem to Jericho, when he fell into the hands of robbers. They stripped him of his clothes, beat him and went away, leaving him half dead. A priest happened to be going down the same road, and when he saw the man, he passed by on the other side. So too, a Levite, when he came to the place and saw him, passed by on the other side. But a Samaritan, as he traveled, came where the man was; and when he saw him, he took pity on him. He went to him and bandaged his wounds, pouring on oil and wine. Then he put the man on his own donkey, took him to an inn and took care of him. The next day he took out two silver coins and gave them to the innkeeper. 'Look after him,' he said, 'and when I return, I will reimburse you for any extra expense you may have.'

"Which of these three do you think was a neighbor to the man who fell into the hands of robbers?"

The expert in the law replied, "The one who had mercy on him."

Jesus told him, "Go and do likewise."

Luke 10:25-37

Faith

Then Caleb silenced the people before Moses and said, "We should go up and take possession of the land, for we can certainly do it."

Numbers 13:30

Even though I walk through the valley of the shadow of death, I will fear no evil, for you are with me; your rod and your staff, they comfort me.

Psalm 23: 4

Say to those with fearful hearts, "Be strong, do not fear; your God will come, he will come with vengeance; with divine retribution he will come to save you."

Isaiah 35: 4

MI tell you the truth, if you have faith as small as a mustard seed, you can say to this mountain, 'Move from here to there' and it will move. Nothing will be impossible for you."

Matthew 17:20b

For nothing is impossible with God."

Luke 1:37

So I say to you: Ask and it will be given to you;
seek and you will find; knock and the door will be
opened to you.

Luke 11:9

Without faith it is impossible to please God, because
anyone who comes to him must believe that he
exists and that he rewards those who earnestly seek
him.

Hebrews 11:6

For everyone born of God overcomes the world.
This is the victory that has overcome the world, even
our faith. . . . This is the confidence we have in
approaching God: that if we ask anything according
to his will, he hears us. And if we know that he
hears us—whatever we ask—we know that we have
what we asked of him.

I John 5:4, 14, 15

Wisdom

I will instruct you and teach you in the way you
should go; I will counsel you and watch over you.

Psalm 32:8

Surely you desire truth in the inner parts; you teach me wisdom in the inmost place.

Psalm 51:6

Then you will understand the fear of the LORD and find the knowledge of God. For the LORD gives wisdom, and from his mouth come knowledge and understanding. He holds victory in store for the upright, he is a shield to those whose walk is blameless.

Proverbs 2:5

To the man who pleases him, God gives wisdom, knowledge and happiness, but to the sinner he gives the task of gathering and storing up wealth to hand it over to the one who pleases God.

Ecclesastes 2:26a

If any of you lacks wisdom, he should ask God, who gives generously to all without finding fault, and it will be given to him.

James 1:5

We know also that the Son of God has come and has given us understanding, so that we may know him who is true. And we are in him who is true—even in his Son Jesus Christ. He is the true God and eternal life.

I John 5:20

Obedience to God

Then he took the Book of the Covenant and read it to the people. They responded, "We will do everything the LORD has said; we will obey."

Exodus 24:7

Love the LORD your God with all your heart and with all your soul and with all your strength.

Deuteronomy 6:5

If my people, who are called by my name, will humble themselves and pray and seek my face and turn from their wicked ways, then will I hear from heaven and will forgive their sin and will heal their land.

II Chronicles 7:14

If they obey and serve him, they will spend the rest of their days in prosperity and their years in contentment..

Job 36:11

May the words of my mouth and the meditation of my heart be pleasing in your sight, O LORD, my Rock and my Redeemer.

Psalm 19:14

But I gave them this command: Obey me, and I will be your God and you will be my people. Walk in all the ways I command you, that it may go well with you.

Jeremiah 7:23

No one can serve two masters. Either he will hate the one and love the other, or he will be devoted to the one and despise the other. You cannot serve both God and Money.

Matthew 6:24

We know that we have come to know him if we obey his commands.

I John 2:3

So whether you eat or drink or whatever you do, do it all for the glory of God.

I Corinthians 10:31

Forgiveness

Do not say, "I'll pay you back for this wrong!" Wait for the LORD, and he will deliver you.

Proverbs 20:22

But I tell you: Love your enemies and pray for those who persecute you, that you may be sons of your Father in heaven. He causes his sun to rise on the evil and the good, and sends rain on the righteous and the unrighteous.

Matthew 5:44, 45

117

For if you forgive men when they sin against you, your heavenly Father will also forgive you.

Matthew 6:14

And when you stand praying, if you hold anything against anyone, forgive him, so that your Father in heaven may forgive you your sins."

Mark 11:25

But love your enemies, do good to them, and lend to them without expecting to get anything back. Then your reward will be great, and you will be sons of the Most High, because he is kind to the ungrateful and wicked. Be merciful, just as your Father is merciful.

"Do not judge, and you will not be judged. Do not condemn, and you will not be condemned. Forgive, and you will be forgiven. Give, and it will be given to you. A good measure, pressed down, shaken together and running over, will be poured into your lap. For with the measure you use, it will be measured to you."

Luke 6:35-38

On the contrary: "If your enemy is hungry, feed him; if he is thirsty, give him something to drink. In doing this, you will heap burning coals on his head."

Romans 12:20

Honesty

Do not steal.
Do not lie.
Do not deceive one another.

Leviticus 19:11

If you sell land to one of your countrymen or buy any from him, do not take advantage of each other. You are to buy from your countryman on the basis of the number of years since the Jubilee. And he is to sell to you on the basis of the number of years left for harvesting crops. When the years are many, you are to increase the price, and when the years are few, you are to decrease the price, because what he is really selling you is the number of crops. Do not take advantage of each other, but fear your God. I am the LORD your God.

Leviticus 25:14-17

You must have accurate and honest weights and measures, so that you may live long in the land the LORD your God is giving you. For the LORD your God detests anyone who does these things, anyone who deals dishonestly.

Deuteronomy 25:15, 16

Keep me from deceitful ways;
be gracious to me through your law.

I have chosen the way of truth;
I have set my heart on your laws.
I hold fast to your statutes, O LORD;
do not let me be put to shame.
I run in the path of your commands,
for you have set my heart free.
Teach me, O LORD, to follow your decrees;
then I will keep them to the end.
Give me understanding,
and I will keep your law and obey it with all my heart.
Direct me in the path of your commands,
for there I find delight.
Turn my heart toward your statutes
and not toward selfish gain.
Turn my eyes away from worthless things;
preserve my life according to your word.

Psalm 119:29-37

Do not lie to each other, since you have taken off your old self with its practices and have put on the new self, which is being renewed in knowledge in the image of its Creator.

Colossians 3:9, 10

Humility

The fear of the LORD teaches a man wisdom, and humility comes before honor.

Proverbs 15:33

Better to be lowly in spirit and among the oppressed than to share plunder with the proud.

Proverbs 16:19

Humility and the fear of the LORD bring wealth and honor and life.

Proverbs 22:4

A man's pride brings him low, but a man of lowly spirit gains honor.

Proverbs 29:23

Therefore, whoever humbles himself like this child is the greatest in the kingdom of heaven.

Matthew 18:4

But he gives us more grace. That is why Scripture says: "God opposes the proud but gives grace to the humble."

James 4:6

Humble yourselves, therefore, under God's mighty hand, that he may lift you up in due time.

I Peter 5:6

Tolerance, Under God's Grace
One man's faith allows him to eat everything, but another man, whose faith is weak, eats only vegetables.

The man who eats everything must not look down on him who does not, and the man who does not eat everything must not condemn the man who does, for God has accepted him. Who are you to judge someone else's servant? To his own master he stands or falls. And he will stand, for the Lord is able to make him stand. One man considers one day more sacred than another; another man considers every day alike.

Each one should be fully convinced in his own mind. He who regards one day as special, does so to the Lord. He who eats meat, eats to the Lord, for he gives thanks to God; and he who abstains, does so to the Lord and gives thanks to God. For none of us lives to himself alone and none of us dies to himself alone. If we live, we live to the Lord; and if we die, we die to the Lord. So, whether we live or die, we belong to the Lord. For this very reason, Christ died and returned to life so that he might be the Lord of both the dead and the living. You, then, why do you judge your brother? Or why do you look down on your brother? For we will all stand before God's judgment seat. It is written: "'As surely as I live,' says the Lord, 'every knee will bow before me; every tongue will confess to God.'" So then, each of us will give an account of himself to God.

Therefore let us stop passing judgment on one another. Instead, make up your mind not to put any stumbling block or obstacle in your brother's way. As one who is in the Lord Jesus, I am fully convinced that no food is unclean in itself. But if anyone regards something as unclean, then for him it is unclean. If your brother is distressed because of what you eat, you are no longer acting in love. Do not by your eating destroy your brother for whom Christ died. Do not allow what you consider good to be spoken of as evil. For the kingdom of God is not a matter of eating and drinking, but of righteousness, peace and joy in the Holy Spirit, So whatever you believe about these things keep between yourself and God. Blessed is the man who does not condemn himself by what he approves.

Romans 14:2-22

It is for freedom that Christ has set us free. Stand firm, then, and do not let yourselves be burdened again by a yoke of slavery.

Galatians 5:1

Peacefulness

Consider the blameless, observe the upright; there is a future for the man of peace.

Psalm 37:37

I will listen to what God the LORD will say; he promises peace to his people, his saints—but let them not return to folly.

Psalm 85:8

123

The fruit of righteousness will be peace; the effect of righteousness will be quietness and confidence forever.

Isaiah 32:17

Peace I leave with you; my peace I give you. I do not give to you as the world gives. Do not let your hearts be troubled and do not be afraid.

John 14:27

Let the peace of Christ rule in your hearts, since as members of one body you were called to peace. And be thankful.

Colossians 3:15

Now may the Lord of peace himself give you peace at all times and in every way. The Lord be with all of you.

II Thessalonians 3:16

FOR PERSONAL PRAYER:

Heavenly Father, help me to know exactly what to teach my kids as I go about their spiritual training. Most of all, though, help me to remember that I am offering to them who I am everyday. Therefore, I want to maintain my personal integrity in every decision that comes my way. Amen.

CHAPTER 7

'How can I make discipline more than just punishment?'

I'll never forget my father telling me about his dad's approach to discipline," said Ed. "You either did what he said, the first time, or you ducked—quick! It used to seem kind of humorous, but now it only gives me a sad feeling. To think that, in his family, discipline came down to having to throw something at a kid to enforce obedience.

"Lately, I've been approaching the task of disciplining my kids as a training venture. I've come to see that offering kids opportunities for accountability and responsibility is the best way to build their self-esteem.

125

I can't *give* them self-esteem, but I can provide the environment for it to blossom."

FOR MEMORY:

Train a child in the way he should go, and when he is old he will not turn from it.

Proverbs 22:6

FOR SILENT REFLECTION:

- *How did my own parents treat me when I disobeyed or disappointed them?*

- *To what degree do I let my anger get the upper hand when correcting my kids?*

- *What responsibilities in the home have I given my children?*

- *In what kinds of situations have I seen the self-esteem of my children blossom the most?*

Train and Instruct Your Children

For I have chosen him, so that he will direct his children and his household after him to keep the way of the LORD by doing what is right and just, so that the LORD will bring about for Abraham what he has promised him.

Genesis 18:19

On that day tell your son, "I do this because of what the LORD did for me when I came out of Egypt."

Exodus 13:8

Only be careful, and watch yourselves closely so that you do not forget the things your eyes have seen or let them slip from your heart as long as you live. Teach them to your children and to their children after them. Remember the day you stood before the LORD your God at Horeb, when he said to me, "Assemble the people before me to hear my words so that they may learn to revere me as long as they live in the land and may teach them to their children."

Deuteronomy 4:9, 10

These commandments that I give you today are to be upon your hearts. Impress them on your children. Talk about them when you sit at home and when you walk along the road, when you lie down and when you get up. Tie them as symbols on your hands and bind them on your foreheads. Write them on the doorframes of your houses and on your gates.

Deuteronomy 6:6-9

Teach them to your children, talking about them when you sit at home and when you walk along the road, when you lie down and when you get up.

Deuteronomy 11:19

I will open my mouth in parables,
I will utter hidden things, things from of old—
what we have heard and known,
what our fathers have told us.
We will not hide them from their children;
we will tell the next generation the praiseworthy deeds of the LORD,
his power, and the wonders he has done.

Psalm 78:2-4

Discipline your son, and he will give you peace; he will bring delight to your soul.

Proverbs 29:17

He who spares the rod hates his son, but he who loves him is careful to discipline him.

Proverbs 13:24

Folly is bound up in the heart of a child, but the rod of discipline will drive it far from him.

Proverbs 22:15

Do not withhold discipline from a child; if you punish him with the rod, he will not die.

Proverbs 23:13

Discipline your son, and he will give you peace; he will bring delight to your soul.

Proverbs 29:17

[A church leader] must manage his own family well and see that his children obey him with proper respect. (If anyone does not know how to manage his own family, how can he take care of God's church?)

I Timothy 3:4

Help Children Recognize Their Duties

Each of you must respect his mother and father, and you must observe my Sabbaths. I am the LORD your God.

Leviticus 19:3

Honor your father and your mother, as the LORD your God has commanded you, so that you may live

129

long and that it may go well with you in the land the
LORD your God is giving you.

Deuteronomy 5:16

My son, keep your father's commands and do not
forsake your mother's teaching.

Proverbs 6:20

A wise son heeds his father's instruction, but a mock-
er does not listen to rebuke.

Proverbs 13:1

A fool spurns his father's discipline, but whoever
heeds correction shows prudence.

Proverbs 15:5

Children, obey your parents in everything, for this
pleases the Lord.

Colossians 3:20

My son, if your heart is wise,
then my heart will be glad;
my inmost being will rejoice
when your lips speak what is right. . . .
Listen to your father, who gave you life,
and do not despise your mother when she is old. . . .
The father of a righteous man has great joy;
he who has a wise son delights in him.

May your father and mother be glad;
may she who gave you birth rejoice!
My son, give me your heart
and let your eyes keep to my ways.

Proverbs 23:15-26

Help Children Submit to God's Discipline

Blessed is the man whom God corrects;
so do not despise the discipline of the Almighty.
For he wounds, but he also binds up;
he injures, but his hands also heal.
From six calamities he will rescue you;
in seven no harm will befall you.
In famine he will ransom you from death,
and in battle from the stroke of the sword.
You will be protected from the lash of the tongue,
and need not fear when destruction comes.
You will laugh at destruction and famine,
and need not fear the beasts of the earth.
For you will have a covenant with the stones of the field,
and the wild animals will be at peace with you.
You will know that your tent is secure;
you will take stock of your property
and find nothing missing.
You will know that your children will be many,
and your descendants like the grass of the earth.

131

You will come to the grave in full vigor,
like sheaves gathered in season.

Job 5:17-26

My son, do not make light of the Lord's discipline,
and do not lose heart when he rebukes you, because
the Lord disciplines those he loves, and he punishes
everyone he accepts as a son.

Endure hardship as discipline; God is treating you
as sons. For what son is not disciplined by his father?
If you are not disciplined (and everyone undergoes
discipline), then you are illegitimate children and not
true sons.

Moreover, we have all had human fathers who
disciplined us and we respected them for it. How
much more should we submit to the Father of our
spirits and live! Our fathers disciplined us for a little
while as they thought best; but God disciplines us for
our good, that we may share in his holiness. No discipline seems pleasant at the time, but painful. Later
on, however, it produces a harvest of righteousness
and peace for those who have been trained by it.

Hebrews 12:5b-11

Help Children Learn to Delay Gratification
He who loves pleasure will become poor; whoever
loves wine and oil will never be rich.

Proverbs 21:17

But mark this: There will be terrible times in the last days. People will be lovers of themselves, lovers of money, boastful, proud, abusive, disobedient to their parents, ungrateful, unholy, without love, unforgiving, slanderous, without self-control, brutal, not lovers of the good, treacherous, rash, conceited, lovers of pleasure rather than lovers of God.

II Timothy 3:1-4

Therefore, prepare your minds for action; be self-controlled; set your hope fully on the grace to be given you when Jesus Christ is revealed. As obedient children, do not conform to the evil desires you had when you lived in ignorance. But just as he who called you is holy, so be holy in all you do; for it is written: "Be holy, because I am holy."

I Peter 1:13-16

Anyone who does not carry his cross and follow me cannot be my disciple. Suppose one of you wants to build a tower. Will he not first sit down and estimate the cost to see if he has enough money to complete it? For if he lays the foundation and is not able to finish it, everyone who sees it will ridicule him, saying, "This fellow began to build and was not able to finish.

Or suppose a king is about to go to war against another king. Will he not first sit down and consider

133

whether he is able with ten thousand men to oppose the one coming against him with twenty thousand? If he is not able, he will send a delegation while the other is still a long way off and will ask for terms of peace. In the same way, any of you who does not give up everything he has cannot be my disciple.

Salt is good, but if it loses its saltiness, how can it be made salty again? It is fit neither for the soil nor for the manure pile; it is thrown out. He who has ears to hear, let him hear."

Luke 14:27-35

That is why I am suffering as I am. Yet I am not ashamed, because I know whom I have believed, and am convinced that he is able to guard what I have entrusted to him for that day.

II Timothy 1:12

Help Children Say NO! to Temptation

What shall we say, then? Shall we go on sinning so that grace may increase? By no means! We died to sin; how can we live in it any longer? Or don't you know that all of us who were baptized into Christ Jesus were baptized into his death? We were therefore buried with him through baptism into death in order that, just as Christ was raised from the dead through the glory of the Father, we too may live a new life.

If we have been united with him like this in his death, we will certainly also be united with him in his resurrection. For we know that our old self was crucified with him so that the body of sin might be done away with, that we should no longer be slaves to sin— because anyone who has died has been freed from sin. . . .

In the same way, count yourselves dead to sin but alive to God in Christ Jesus. Therefore do not let sin reign in your mortal body so that you obey its evil desires.

Romans 6:1-7, 11, 12

No temptation has seized you except what is common to man. And God is faithful; he will not let you be tempted beyond what you can bear. But when you are tempted, he will also provide a way out so that you can stand up under it.

I Corinthians 10:13

Finally, be strong in the Lord and in his mighty power. Put on the full armor of God so that you can take your stand against the devil's schemes. For our struggle is not against flesh and blood, but against the rulers, against the authorities, against the powers of this dark world and against the spiritual forces of

135

evil in the heavenly realms.

Therefore put on the full armor of God, so that when the day of evil comes, you may be able to stand your ground, and after you have done everything, to stand.

Stand firm then, with the belt of truth buckled around your waist, with the breastplate of righteousness in place, and with your feet fitted with the readiness that comes from the gospel of peace. In addition to all this, take up the shield of faith, with which you can extinguish all the flaming arrows of the evil one. Take the helmet of salvation and the sword of the Spirit, which is the word of God.

And pray in the Spirit on all occasions with all kinds of prayers and requests. With this in mind, be alert and always keep on praying for all the saints.

Ephesians 6:10-18

But the Lord is faithful, and he will strengthen and protect you from the evil one.

II Thessalonians 3:3

Be self-controlled and alert. Your enemy the devil prowls around like a roaring lion looking for someone to devour. Resist him, standing firm in the faith, because you know that your brothers throughout the world are undergoing the same kind of sufferings. And the God of all grace, who called you to his eternal glory in Christ, after you have suffered a little while, will himself restore you and make you strong, firm and steadfast.

I Peter 5:8-10

Help Children Make the Right Choices

This day I call heaven and earth as witnesses against you that I have set before you life and death, blessings and curses. Now choose life, so that you and your children may live.

Deuteronomy 30:19

But if serving the LORD seems undesirable to you, then choose for yourselves this day whom you will serve, whether the gods your forefathers served beyond the River, or the gods of the Amorites, in whose land you are living. But as for me and my household, we will serve the LORD."

Joshua 24:15

Then David said to God, "I have sinned greatly by doing this. Now, I beg you, take away the guilt of your servant. I have done a very foolish thing." The LORD said to Gad, David's seer, "Go and tell David, 'This is what the LORD says: I am giving you three options. Choose one of them for me to carry out against you."

So Gad went to David and said to him, "This is what the LORD says: 'Take your choice: three years of famine, three months of being swept away before your enemies, with their swords overtaking you, or three days of the sword of the LORD—days of plague in the land, with the angel of the LORD ravaging every part of Israel.'

Now then, decide how I should answer the one who sent me." David said to Gad, "I am in deep distress. Let me fall into the hands of the LORD, for his mercy is very great; but do not let me fall into the hands of men."

I Chronicles 21:8-13

Help Children Develop Accountability

He who heeds discipline shows the way to life, but whoever ignores correction leads others astray.

Proverbs 10:17

He who scorns instruction will pay for it, but he who respects a command is rewarded.

Proverbs 13:13

The faithless will be fully repaid for their ways, and the good man rewarded for his.

Proverbs 14:14

He who listens to a life-giving rebuke will be at home among the wise. He who ignores discipline despises himself, but whoever heeds correction gains understanding. The fear of the LORD teaches a man wisdom, and humility comes before honor.

Proverbs 15:31-33

A man's pride brings him low, but a man of lowly spirit gains honor.

Proverbs 29:23

To Authorities

Everyone must submit himself to the governing authorities, for there is no authority except that which God has established. The authorities that exist have been established by God. Consequently, he who rebels against the authority is rebelling against what God has instituted, and those who do so will bring judgment on themselves. For rulers hold no terror for those who do right, but for those who do wrong. Do you want to be free from fear of the one in authority?

Then do what is right and he will commend you. For he is God's servant to do you good. But if you do wrong, be afraid, for he does not bear the sword for nothing. He is God's servant, an agent of wrath to bring punishment on the wrongdoer. Therefore, it is necessary to submit to the authorities, not only

139

because of possible punishment but also because of conscience. This is also why you pay taxes, for the authorities are God's servants, who give their full time to governing. Give everyone what you owe him: If you owe taxes, pay taxes; if revenue, then revenue; if respect, then respect; if honor, then honor. Let no debt remain outstanding, except the continuing debt to love one another, for he who loves his fellowman has fulfilled the law. . . .

Let us behave decently, as in the daytime, not in orgies and drunkenness, not in sexual immorality and debauchery, not in dissension and jealousy. Rather, clothe yourselves with the Lord Jesus Christ, and do not think about how to gratify the desires of the sinful nature.

Romans 13:1-8, 13, 14

In Their Choice of Friends

Blessed is the man who does not walk
in the counsel of the wicked
or stand in the way of sinners
or sit in the seat of mockers.
But his delight is in the law of the LORD,
and on his law he meditates day and night.

Psalm 1:1, 2

A righteous man is cautious in friendship, but the way of the wicked leads them astray.

Proverbs 12:26

A perverse man stirs up dissension, and a gossip separates close friends.

Proverbs 16:28

A man of many companions may come to ruin, but there is a friend who sticks closer than a brother.

Proverbs 18:24

Do not make friends with a hot-tempered man, do not associate with one easily angered.

Proverbs 22:24

Wounds from a friend can be trusted,
but an enemy multiplies kisses.

Proverbs 27:6

If one falls down, his friend can help him up. But pity the man who falls and has no one to help him up!

Ecclesiastes 4:10

In Their Responsibilities

I went past the field of the sluggard,
past the vineyard of the man who lacks judgment;
thorns had come up everywhere,

141

the ground was covered with weeds,
and the stone wall was in ruins.
I applied my heart to what I observed
and learned a lesson from what I saw:
A little sleep, a little slumber,
a little folding of the hands to rest—
and poverty will come on you like a bandit
and scarcity like an armed man.

Proverbs 24:30-34

Do you not know that in a race all the runners run, but only one gets the prize? Run in such a way as to get the prize. Everyone who competes in the games goes into strict training. They do it to get a crown that will not last; but we do it to get a crown that will last forever. Therefore I do not run like a man running aimlessly; I do not fight like a man beating the air. No, I beat my body and make it my slave so that after I have preached to others, I myself will not be disqualified for the prize.

I Corinthians 9:24-27

Mind your own business and work with your hands, just as we told you, so that your daily life may win the respect of outsiders and so that you will not be dependent on anybody.

I Thessalonians 4:11b, 12

For even when we were with you, we gave you this rule: "If a man will not work, he shall not eat." We hear that some among you are idle. They are not busy; they are busybodies.

Such people we command and urge in the Lord Jesus Christ to settle down and earn the bread they eat.

II Thessalonians 3:10-12

To Their Lord

"Not everyone who says to me, 'Lord, Lord,' will enter the kingdom of heaven, but only he who does the will of my Father who is in heaven. Many will say to me on that day, 'Lord, Lord, did we not prophesy in your name, and in your name drive out demons and perform many miracles?' Then I will tell them plainly, 'I never knew you. Away from me, you evildoers!' "Therefore everyone who hears these words of mine and puts them into practice is like a wise man who built his house on the rock. The rain came down, the streams rose, and the winds blew and beat against that house; yet it did not fall, because it had its foundation on the rock. But everyone who hears these words of mine and does not put them into practice is like a foolish man who built his house on sand. The rain came down, the streams rose, and the winds blew and beat against that house, and it fell with a great crash." When Jesus had finished saying these

143

things, the crowds were amazed at his teaching.

Matthew 7:21-28

Do not merely listen to the word, and so deceive yourselves. Do what it says. Anyone who listens to the word but does not do what it says is like a man who looks at his face in a mirror and, after looking at himself, goes away and immediately forgets what he looks like. But the man who looks intently into the perfect law that gives freedom, and continues to do this, not forgetting what he has heard, but doing it— he will be blessed in what he does. If anyone considers himself religious and yet does not keep a tight rein on his tongue, he deceives himself and his religion is worthless. Religion that God our Father accepts as pure and faultless is this: to look after orphans and widows in their distress and to keep oneself from being polluted by the world.

James 1:22-27

FOR PERSONAL PRAYER:

Lord, keep reminding me that discipline is more than punishment, that it's a whole life of loving training. Keep me open to ways I can place trust in my kids. And give me the grace to forgive and restore them when they fail. Amen.

CHAPTER 8

'How can I handle my frustrations with this incredible parenting challenge?'

S ometimes it's just too much," said Jerry. "I've had times when I thought I was going to blow my top."

"You see, I come home from a job that is nothing but pressure, pressure, pressure, nine or ten hours each day. At the end of one of those days, I walk into the living room hoping to relax a little and I get hit, first thing, with the kid-crisis of the day. It's always something; always something to keep the family up in the air. Sometimes I just feel like giving up."

FOR MEMORY:

Let us not become weary in doing good, for at the proper time we will reap a harvest if we do not give up.

Galatians 6:9

FOR SILENT REFLECTION:

- *How hard is it for me to admit that I'm hurting or need help?*

- *When did I last share my hurts and frustrations with my wife?*

- *What do I do with my anger when it starts to boil over?*

- *How could I begin to see frustration as a call to rely more on God's strength?*

Feeling Tired and Worn Down?

Be merciful to me, LORD, for I am faint; O LORD, heal me, for my bones are in agony.

Psalm 6:2

Show me, O LORD,
my life's end and the number of my days;
let me know how fleeting is my life.
You have made my days a mere handbreadth;
the span of my years is as nothing before you.
Each man's life is but a breath.

Psalm 39:4, 5

I have seen something else under the sun:
The race is not to the swift
or the battle to the strong,
nor does food come to the wise
or wealth to the brilliant o
r favor to the learned;
but time and chance happen to them all.
Moreover, no man knows when his hour will come:
As fish are caught in a cruel net,
or birds are taken in a snare,
so men are trapped by evil times
that fall unexpectedly upon them.

Ecclesiastes 9:11, 12

All men are like grass, and all their glory is like the flowers of the field.

Isaiah 40:6b

But God chose the foolish things of the world to shame the wise; God chose the weak things of the world to shame the strong.

1 Corinthians 1:27

That is why, for Christ's sake, I delight in weaknesses, in insults, in hardships, in persecutions, in difficulties. For when I am weak, then I am strong.

2 Corinthians 12:10

But we have this treasure in jars of clay to show that this all-surpassing power is from God and not from us. We are hard pressed on every side, but not crushed; perplexed, but not in despair; persecuted, but not abandoned; struck down, but not destroyed. We always carry around in our body the death of Jesus, so that the life of Jesus may also be revealed in our body. For we who are alive are always being given over to death for Jesus' sake, so that his life may be revealed in our mortal body.

II Corinthians 4:7-11

I lift up my eyes to the hills—
where does my help come from?
My help comes from the LORD,
the Maker of heaven and earth.
He will not let your foot slip—
he who watches over you will not slumber;
indeed, he who watches over Israel
will neither slumber nor sleep.
The LORD watches over you—
the LORD is your shade at your right hand;
the sun will not harm you by day,
nor the moon by night.
The LORD will keep you from all harm—
he will watch over your life;
the LORD will watch over your coming and going
both now and forevermore.

Psalm 121:1-8

Feeling Afraid?

Be strong and courageous. Do not be afraid or terrified because of them, for the LORD your God goes with you; he will never leave you nor forsake you.

Deuteronomy 31:6

Have I not commanded you? Be strong and courageous. Do not be terrified; do not be discouraged, for the LORD your God will be with you wherever you go.

Joshua 1:9

Though an army besiege me, my heart will not fear; though war break out against me, even then will I be confident.

Psalm 27:3

Therefore we will not fear, though the earth give way and the mountains fall into the heart of the sea.

Psalm 46:2

Whoever listens to me will live in safety and be at ease, without fear of harm.

Proverbs 1:33

For God did not give us a spirit of timidity, but a spirit of power, of love and of self-discipline.

II Timothy 1:7

There is no fear in love. But perfect love drives out fear, because fear has to do with punishment. The one who fears is not made perfect in love.

I John 4:18

Feeling Angry and Frustrated?

The LORD God provided a vine and made it grow up over Jonah to give shade for his head to ease his discomfort, and Jonah was very happy about the vine. But at dawn the next day God provided a worm, which chewed the vine so that it withered. When the sun rose, God provided a scorching east wind, and the sun blazed on Jonah's head so that he grew faint. He wanted to die, and said, "It would be better for me to die than to live."

But God said to Jonah, "Do you have a right to be angry about the vine?"

"I do," he said. "I am angry enough to die."

Jonah 4:6-9

In your anger do not sin; when you are on your beds, search your hearts and be silent.

Psalm 4:4

But I tell you that anyone who is angry with his brother will be subject to judgment. Again, anyone who says to his brother, 'Raca,' is answerable to the Sanhedrin. But anyone who says, 'You fool!' will be in danger of the fire of hell.

Matthew 5:22

151

Do not let the sun go down while you are still angry.
Ephesians 4:26b

Do not seek revenge or bear a grudge against one of your people, but love your neighbor as yourself. I am the LORD.
Leviticus 19:18

Get rid of all bitterness, rage and anger, brawling and slander, along with every form of malice.
Ephesians 4:31

See to it that no one misses the grace of God and that no bitter root grows up to cause trouble and defile many.
Hebrews 12:15

Feeling Worried?

I tell you, do not worry about your life, what you will eat or drink; or about your body, what you will wear. Is not life more important than food, and the body more important than clothes? Look at the birds of the air; they do not sow or reap or store away in barns, and yet your heavenly Father feeds them. Are you not much more valuable than they? Who of you by worrying can add a single hour to his life? And why do you worry about clothes? See how the lilies of the field grow. They do not labor or spin. Yet I tell you that not even Solomon in all his splendor was dressed like one of these. If that is how God clothes the grass of the field, which is here today and tomorrow is thrown into the fire, will he not much more clothe you, O you of little faith? So do not worry, saying, "What shall we eat?" or "What shall we drink?" or "What shall we wear?"

For the pagans run after all these things, and your heavenly Father knows that you need them. But seek first his kingdom and his righteousness, and all these things will be given to you as well. Therefore do not worry about tomorrow, for tomorrow will worry about itself. Each day has enough trouble of its own.

Matthew 6:25-34

Do not be anxious about anything, but in everything, by prayer and petition, with thanksgiving, present your requests to God. And the peace of God, which transcends all understanding, will guard your hearts and your minds in Christ Jesus. I am not saying this because I am in need, for I have learned to be content whatever the circumstances. I know what it is to be in need, and I know what it is to have plenty. I have learned the secret of being content in any and every situation, whether well fed or hungry, whether living in plenty or in want.

Philippians 4:6-12

Feeling Discouraged and Like a Failure?

I am worn out from groaning; all night long I flood my bed with weeping and drench my couch with tears.

Psalm 6:6

How long, O LORD?
Will you forget me forever?
How long will you hide your face from me?

Psalm 13:1

My disgrace is before me all day long, and my face is covered with shame.

Psalm 44:15

Scorn has broken my heart and has left me helpless; I looked for sympathy, but there was none, for comforters, but I found none.

Psalm 69:20

I know that nothing good lives in me, that is, in my sinful nature. For I have the desire to do what is good, but I cannot carry it out. For what I do is not the good I want to do; no, the evil I do not want to do—this I keep on doing. Now if I do what I do not want to do, it is no longer I who do it, but it is sin living in me that does it.

Romans 7:18-20

The LORD is close to the brokenhearted and saves those who are crushed in spirit.

Psalm 34:18

I will exalt you, O LORD,
for you lifted me out of the depths
and did not let my enemies gloat over me.
O LORD my God, I called to you for help
and you healed me.
O LORD, you brought me up from the grave;
you spared me from going down into the pit.
Sing to the LORD, you saints of his;
praise his holy name.
For his anger lasts only a moment,
but his favor lasts a lifetime;
weeping may remain for a night,
but rejoicing comes in the morning.

Psalm 30:1-5

Cast your cares on the LORD and he will sustain you;
he will never let the righteous fall.

Psalm 55:22

He heals the brokenhearted and binds up their wounds.

Psalm 147:3

When you pass through the waters, I will be with you; and when you pass through the rivers, they will not sweep over you. When you walk through the fire, you will not be burned; the flames will not set you ablaze.

Isaiah 43:2

Only God Is Perfect

He is the Rock, his works are perfect, and all his ways are just. A faithful God who does no wrong, upright and just is he.

Deuteronomy 32:4

As for God, his way is perfect; the word of the LORD is flawless. He is a shield for all who take refuge in him.

II Samuel 22:312

But he said to me, "My grace is sufficient for you, for my power is made perfect in weakness." Therefore I will boast all the more gladly about my weaknesses, so that Christ's power may rest on me.

II Corinthians 12:9

Can You Accept Your Limitations?

Show me, O LORD, my life's end and the number of my days; let me know how fleeting is my life.

Psalms 39:4

If anyone thinks he is something when he is nothing, he deceives himself.

Galatians 6:3

Come to me, all you who are weary and burdened, and I will give you rest. Take my yoke upon you and learn from me, for I am gentle and humble in heart, and you will find rest for your souls. For my yoke is easy and my burden is light.

Matthew 11:28-30

Finally, be strong in the Lord and in his mighty power.

Ephesians 6:10

Have You Sought God's Peace?

You will keep in perfect peace him whose mind is steadfast, because he trusts in you.

Isaiah 26:3

He will be like a tree planted by the water that sends out its roots by the stream. It does not fear when heat comes; its leaves are always green. It has no worries in a year of drought and never fails to bear fruit.

Jeremiah 17:8

Peace I leave with you; my peace I give you. I do not give to you as the world gives. Do not let your hearts be troubled and do not be afraid.

John 14:27

I have told you these things, so that in me you may have peace. In this world you will have trouble. But take heart! I have overcome the world.

John 16:33

For God is not a God of disorder but of peace. As in all the congregations of the saints.

I Corinthians 14:33

Now may the Lord of peace himself give you peace at all times and in every way. The Lord be with all of you.

II Thessalonians 3:16

FOR PERSONAL PRAYER:

Lord, help me to handle my frustrations in ways that model Your values before my children. Give me the courage to admit—to You and to my wife—when I'm hurting or need help. Amen.

CHAPTER 9

'How can I hold onto the joy of being a dad in the midst of home and work and stresses?'

I've heard that stress is a killer," said Myron. "So I know I've got to figure out a way to beat it. I'm trying to eat better and make time for more exercise, as well as getting plenty of rest.

"I'm tempted to think these are selfish things, but I know that the better shape I'm in—physically, emotionally, and spiritually—the better fathering I have to offer my children. It takes loads of energy to be a loving parent. And I'm going to do everything I can to keep that inward energy level high so my love can keep flowing outward."

FOR MEMORY:

[The Father] comforts us in all our troubles, so that we can comfort those in any trouble with the comfort we ourselves have received from God.

II Corinthians 1:4

FOR SILENT REFLECTION:

- *How well have I been taking care of myself lately?*

- *Do I view my own physical and emotional maintenance as a means of loving my children?*

- *What self-destructive attitudes or habits can I ask God to help me conquer?*

Dealing with Your Home and Work Stresses

When Dad Is Content with His Work

Then I realized that it is good and proper for a man to eat and drink, and to find satisfaction in his toilsome labor under the sun during the few days of life God has given him—for this is his lot. Moreover, when God gives any man wealth and possessions, and enables him to enjoy them, to accept his lot and be happy in his work—this is a gift of God.

-Ecclesiastes 5:18, 19

When Dad Is Content at Home

LORD, you have assigned me my portion and my cup; you have made my lot secure.

Psalm 16:5

The boundary lines have fallen for me in pleasant places; surely I have a delightful inheritance.

Proverbs 16:5, 6

Delight yourself in the LORD and he will give you the desires of your heart.

Psalm 37:4

Better a meal of vegetables where there is love than a fattened calf with hatred.

Proverbs 15:17

By wisdom a house is built,
and through understanding it is established;
through knowledge its rooms are filled
with rare and beautiful treasures.

Proverbs 24:3, 4

The LORD will guide you always; he will satisfy your needs in a sun-scorched land and will strengthen your frame. You will be like a well-watered garden, like a spring whose waters never fail.

Isaiah 58:11

Taking Time for Rest and Renewal
Six days do your work, but on the seventh day do not work, so that your ox and your donkey may rest and the slave born in your household, and the alien as well, may be refreshed.

Exodus 23:12

The apostles gathered around Jesus and reported to him all they had done and taught. Then, because so many people were coming and going that they did not even have a chance to eat, he said to them, "Come with me by yourselves to a quiet place and get some rest." So they went away by themselves in a boat to a solitary place.

Mark 6:30-32

162

Maintaining Your Spiritual Health

Asking God to Meet Your Needs

Ask of me, and I will make the nations your inheritance, the ends of the earth your possession.

Psalm 2:8

This is what the LORD says: "Stand at the crossroads and look; ask for the ancient paths, ask where the good way is, and walk in it, and you will find rest for your souls. But you said, "We will not walk in it."

Jeremiah 6:16

Ask the LORD for rain in the springtime; it is the LORD who makes the storm clouds. He gives showers of rain to men, and plants of the field to everyone.

Zechariah 10:1

Again, I tell you that if two of you on earth agree about anything you ask for, it will be done for you by my Father in heaven.

Matthew 18:19

If you believe, you will receive whatever you ask for in prayer.

Matthew 21:22

163

Until now you have not asked for anything in my name. Ask and you will receive, and your joy will be complete.

John 16:24

This is the confidence we have in approaching God: that if we ask anything according to his will, he hears us. And if we know that he hears us—whatever we ask—we know that we have what we asked of him.

I John 5:14, 15

Now to him who is able to do immeasurably more than all we ask or imagine, according to his power that is at work within us.

Ephesians 3:20

Finding Comfort through Friends and Other Christians

How good and pleasant it is
when brothers live together in unity!
It is like precious oil poured on the head,
running down on the beard,
running down on Aaron's beard,
down upon the collar of his robes.
It is as if the dew of Hermon were falling on Mount Zion.
For there the LORD bestows his blessing,
even life forevermore.

Psalm 133:1-3

Be devoted to one another in brotherly love. Honor one another above yourselves.

Romans 12:10

Therefore encourage one another and build each other up, just as in fact you are doing. . . . And we urge you, brothers, warn those who are idle, encourage the timid, help the weak, be patient with everyone.

I Thessalonians 5:11, 14

Let us not give up meeting together, as some are in the habit of doing, but let us encourage one another—and all the more as you see the Day approaching.

Hebrews 10:25

The body is a unit, though it is made up of many parts; and though all its parts are many, they form one body. So it is with Christ. For we were all baptized by one Spirit into one body—whether Jews or Greeks, slave or free—and we were all given the one Spirit to drink.

Now the body is not made up of one part but of many. If the foot should say, "Because I am not a hand, I do not belong to the body," it would not for that reason cease to be part of the body.

And if the ear should say, "Because I am not an

165

eye, I do not belong to the body," it would not for that reason cease to be part of the body. If the whole body were an eye, where would the sense of hearing be? If the whole body were an ear, where would the sense of smell be?

But in fact God has arranged the parts in the body, every one of them, just as he wanted them to be. If they were all one part, where would the body be? As it is, there are many parts, but one body. The eye cannot say to the hand, "I don't need you!" And the head cannot say to the feet, "I don't need you!"

On the contrary, those parts of the body that seem to be weaker are indispensable, and the parts that we think are less honorable we treat with special honor. And the parts that are unpresentable are treated with special modesty, while our presentable parts need no special treatment. But God has combined the members of the body and has given greater honor to the parts that lacked it, so that there should be no division in the body, but that its parts should have equal concern for each other.

If one part suffers, every part suffers with it; if one part is honored, every part rejoices with it.

I Corinthians 12:12-26

They devoted themselves to the apostles' teaching and to the fellowship, to the breaking of bread and to prayer. Everyone was filled with awe, and many wonders and miraculous signs were done by the apostles. All the believers were together and had everything in common. Selling their possessions and goods, they gave to anyone as he had need.

Every day they continued to meet together in the temple courts. They broke bread in their homes and ate together with glad and sincere hearts, praising God and enjoying the favor of all the people. And the Lord added to their number daily those who were being saved.

Acts 2:42-47

There is one body and one Spirit—just as you were called to one hope when you were called—one Lord, one faith, one baptism; one God and Father of all, who is over all and through all and in all.

Ephesians 4:4-6

If anyone says, "I love God," yet hates his brother, he is a liar. For anyone who does not love his brother, whom he has seen, cannot love God, whom he has not seen. And he has given us this command: Whoever loves God must also love his brother.

I John 4:20, 21

Lifting Your Spirit with Praise to God
I will praise you, O LORD, with all my heart;
I will tell of all your wonders.

I will be glad and rejoice in you;
I will sing praise to your name, O Most High.
My enemies turn back;
they stumble and perish before you.
For you have upheld my right and my cause;
you have sat on your throne, judging righteously.
You have rebuked the nations
and destroyed the wicked;
you have blotted out their name for ever and ever.

Psalm 9:1-5

Sing joyfully to the LORD, you righteous;
it is fitting for the upright to praise him.
Praise the LORD with the harp;
make music to him on the ten-stringed lyre.
Sing to him a new song; play skillfully,
and shout for joy.
For the word of the LORD is right and true;
he is faithful in all he does. The LORD loves righteousness and justice;
the earth is full of his unfailing love.

Psalm 33:1-5

Shout with joy to God, all the earth!
Sing the glory of his name; make his praise glorious!
Say to God, "How awesome are your deeds!
So great is your power
that your enemies cringe before you.